VGM Opportunities Series

OPPORTUNITIES IN
NUTRITION CAREERS

Carol Coles Caldwell

Revised by
Marguerite Duffy

VGM Career Horizons
NTC/Contemporary Publishing Group

Library of Congress Cataloging-in-Publication Data

Caldwell, Carol C. (Carol Coles)
    Opportunities in nutrition careers / Carol Coles Caldwell.
        p.   cm. — (VGM opportunities series)
    Previously published in 1992.
    Includes bibliographical references.
    ISBN (invalid) 0-8442-3240-2 (cloth). — ISBN 0-8442-3251-3 (pbk.)
    1. Dietetics Vocational guidance.   I. Title.   II. Series.
    [RM218.5. C35   1999]
    613.2'023'73—DC21   99-34064
                                                                    CIP

Cover photographs: © PhotoDisc, Inc.

Published by VGM Career Horizons
A division of NTC/Contemporary Publishing Group, Inc.
4255 West Touhy Avenue, Lincolnwood (Chicago), Illinois 60712-1975 U.S.A.
Copyright © 2000 by NTC/Contemporary Publishing Group, Inc.
Printed in the United States of America
International Standard Book Number: 0-8442-3240-2 (cloth)
                                                          0-8442-3251-3 (paper)
    00   01   02   03   04   LB   18   17   16   15   14   13   12   11   10 9   8   7   6   5   4   3   2

CONTENTS

ABOUT THE AUTHOR

Carol Caldwell is a graduate of the University of Arizona in Tucson, where she received her bachelor's degree in 1980 and master's in 1981, both in nutritional sciences. In 1986, she graduated from Peter Kump's New York Cooking School, where she developed a foundation in French cooking techniques. This enabled her to combine the disciplines of cooking and nutrition.

In 1983, Ms. Caldwell managed the nutrition department at Canyon Ranch Spa Resort in Tucson, Arizona. She then went to Miami, Florida, in 1986 to develop the nutrition and food program for the Doral Saturnia Spa. Ms. Caldwell returned to New York City as a nutrition and food consultant in 1987. As a consultant, she has taught Spa Cuisine cooking classes at Peter Kump's New York Cooking School; developed nutritional software for Nutridata Software Corporation; advised Children's Television Workshop on the nutritive quality of proposed Sesame Street brand children's snack foods; developed healthy menus for restaurants; and catered nutritional cuisine for private parties in New York. In addition, Carol Caldwell has written articles for major magazines such as *New Woman, New Body,* and *Mademoiselle.* In 1993, she collaborated with the Culinary Institute of America to write *The Professional Chef's Techniques of Healthy Cooking.*

Ms. Caldwell worked as a consultant with Commercial Aluminum Cookware Company, the makers of Calphalon cookware. She developed recipes for use in promotions, cooking classes, and bro-chures. In addition, Ms. Caldwell created recipes for American Spoon Foods, a specialty food company located in Petosky, Michigan.]

   This edition was revised by Marguerite Duffy, a writer/editor of career books.

FOREWORD

Nutritionists, of course, have always known that good dietary habits are key to good health. The old adage "You are what you eat" is familiar to everyone, but in recent decades, the public has begun to take those words very seriously, realizing that the body (and the mind) is only as good as the food that fuels it.

As interest in good nutrition and diet increased, so did the number of specialties and subspecialties within this field. But what is a sound, healthy diet for one person, may have little benefit for another. It all depends on an individual's health, cultural background, eating habits, environment, etc. Only a professional in nutrition can assemble and interpret all the dieting and health data about an individual and create a reasonable and healthful meal plan for him or her.

Opportunities in Nutrition Careers defines nutrition, explains and explores the various roles of dietitians, and provides information on salaries and job satisfaction. It is an excellent primer to this rapidly growing, exciting field.

The Editors
VGM Career Books

INTRODUCTION

The nutritionist and the dietitian are concerned with providing nutrition-related services to people. The dietitian is considered a health care professional, who may hold credentials as a registered dietitian, who affects the nutritional care of individuals and groups in health and illness.

The work of the dietitian and the nutritionist includes the application of the science and art of human nutrition in helping people select and obtain food for the primary purpose of nourishing their bodies in health or disease throughout their life cycles. The professional's participation may include client nutritional assessment and intervention, nutrition education, consultation to food service and management, corporate health promotion, research, and food product/recipe development.

NUTRITION AS A SCIENCE AND AN ART

To understand the scope of the profession, it is important to define the terms *nutrition* and *nutritional care*. These are terms that help to describe how a dietitian may choose to practice in various areas.

Nutrition is defined today as the science of food, the nutrients and other substances therein, their action, interaction, and balance in relation to health and disease, and the process by which humans ingest, digest, absorb, transport, utilize, and excrete food substances. In addition, nutrition must be concerned with social, economic, cultural, and psychological implications of food and eating.

Nutritional care is the application of the science of nutrition. It is the art of helping people select and obtain food for the primary purpose of nourishing their bodies. It is essential both in health and disease throughout the life cycle.

The goals of nutritional care are comprehensive. They include improvement of the quality of life, prevention of disease, and clinical therapy during illness. To meet the goals of nutritional care dietitians practice in many different settings: hospitals or other health care facilities; schools and universities; business and industry; foodservice operations including restaurants, food chains, airlines, and spas; and community agencies. Dietetic practitioners can be involved in clinical practice, research, management of foodservice systems, food processing, cooking, communications (TV, radio, newspapers, magazines, computers, public relations, etc.), and teaching. Whether nutritional care is provided to improve the lives of individuals, manage a large-scale food operation, teach other health scientists and consumers, or explain the nutritive content of food to children, the dietitian will be participating in many sophisticated and multifaceted roles.

THE EXPANDING ROLE OF NUTRITION

The role of nutritionists and dietitians in our society is in a state of rapid growth and change. Only a few short years ago, the most basic principles of nutrition were largely unknown to the general public. Today, knowledge of the role of nutrition in human health is increasingly the subject of magazine and newspaper articles, books, television shows, and programs at public meetings. Movie stars, presidents, and other public personalities mention their health and fitness activities. Athletes are quoted on how they maintain their diets and nutritional well-being.

Interest in nutrition is depicted in food product commercials and in newspaper and magazine advertising. Demand for nutritional information on packaged food products has created a new policy, and product labels are increasingly specific about the nutritional value of the products. Hospitals, doctors, and nurses are greatly concerned about nutrition, and many have returned to medical schools for the latest information on nutrition and dietetics.

Nutrition courses in public schools, colleges, medical schools, and other educational institutions are on the rise. The result of all this growth has been a flurry of new, widely varied, exciting courses available to the public and to the nutrition specialist.

THE PROFESSIONAL OUTLOOK

To the person who is presently considering a career as a nutrition professional, a dietitian, a nutritionist, a teacher, a writer, a consultant, or a nutrition therapist, or any of a number of new specialties in this area, this is a time of increasingly new opportunities. As the nutrition field grows in the next decade, more and more positions will open up. For some, this period of growth and change will actually mean pioneering in areas of human nutritional care that have not even been imagined today. Just as the health spa is no longer the privilege of only a few, good nutritional practices are no longer within the reach of only the privileged. The public is growing more and more aware of the opportunities for better health and longer life through the use of good nutritional practices—and the demand for professionals in this field will continue to expand along with this public awareness.

CHAPTER 1

AN EXCITING AND CHALLENGING PROFESSION: NUTRITION

It is a wonderful time to be a nutrition professional. Never before have so many people been so visibly interested in nutrition. Popular interest in this subject can be measured by the large number of bestseller diet books, as well as the fortunes being made by serving the public's desire for nutritional information and diet counseling, health books, and diet supplements.

It is now apparent that optimal nutrition can be a strong factor in maintaining health and preventing disease. Physicians and other health professionals—as well as corporate presidents, chefs, and major foodservice operators—recognize the value of nutrition. The complexities of modern medicine demand high-quality nutritional care, while the general public demands nutritional food.

CHANGES IN THE FIELD

Dramatic changes are occurring in the nutrition profession. These changes arise from two new developments: (1) computer applications in the nutrition field; and (2) the general population's desire to know more about how nutrition affects them as individuals. The success of this field's expansion relies on the dietitian's ability to provide quality services to the public, at a time when the public is searching for accurate nutritional information and cost-effective health care.

Opportunities are available to the nutrition professional to expand the practice environment. Dietitians may act as consultants to small community hospitals, long-term nursing care institutions, or special interest groups, such as sports trainers. In industry, they may be members of a product development or market research team, or they may be in the sales force. In public health, they may supervise nutritional programs for the elderly or for patients recently released from acute-care facilities. In food service, they may work with a chef to develop healthy recipes and help to determine a marketing plan. In the community, the dietitian may provide nutritional support or outpatient and in-home counseling services.

BEFORE YOU ENTER THIS PROFESSION

Before entering this job market, it is critical to determine your individual interests. Dietitians in different types of settings have different types of experiences. Therefore, you should consider what kind of experience you want before searching for a position. Consult the phone directory in your area for nutritionist listings. Call one and ask to set up an interview. You can quickly gain an insight into the profession by talking with nutritionists and dietitians in the field (see also Chapter 13 for interviews with current practitioners).

The challenges the nutrition professional faces are exciting. It is a time when nutrition experts can create the world in which they work, but it will take initiative, advanced knowledge, and the development of individual expertise. As a nutrition professional, you will find it a privilege to play a crucial role in this field; for nutrition is an essential component, not only of health and health care, but of life itself.

CHAPTER 2

THE DIETITIAN'S HERITAGE: THE AMERICAN DIETETIC ASSOCIATION

The profession of "Dietetics," as it is known today, began with the founding of the American Dietetic Association in 1917, under the direction of Lenna Frances Copper. She believed that there was a need for a conference to formulate a plan for dietetic communication. The first challenge faced by this new organization was how dietitians could best serve the nation's needs during World War I, both at home and overseas.

ADMINISTRATION AND MANAGEMENT

Originally, administrative dietetics and food management were the specialties of the profession. The term *dietitian* was associated with those who worked in hospitals. Their objective was to provide quantity food production without loss of quality, and to standardize institutional feeding.

DEVELOPMENT OF STANDARDS

During the second decade of the association, the dietitian was involved with support of government regulation and welfare agencies, food labeling, development of labor standards for commercial food service, and development of hospital food service plans. This dietetic movement was described as "one of the greatest existing forces in the promotion of health and the prevention of disease,"[1] but real advances would be achieved only when the results of nutritional research could be integrated into the practices of the population.

By the 1940s, it had become clear that the profession needed to further develop standards in monitoring the quality of food and to become involved in research to develop new food products. In addition, dietitians were involved in government efforts to develop nutritional standards for the school lunch programs.

PUBLIC INFORMATION

During the 1950s, the American Dietetic Association began a formal public relations program to strengthen the position of the dietitian and to promote better understanding and recognition of the expertise of the dietitian. Dietitians were also urged to contribute to national health, research, and education. They were no longer involved in only foodservice and quality control but were expanding into all areas that nutrition could affect. These areas included government agencies, food industries, universities and schools, and public health education.

NEW METHODS, EDUCATION, AND RESEARCH

The next decade was a time for the dietitian to seek new methods and adapt to changing conditions, a challenge that carried into

---

1. Turner, C. E.: Health Education as a World Movement. *J. Am. Diet. Assoc.* 12:457, 1936.

each subsequent decade as the dietitian continued to search for new information and improve the quality of life through nutrition.

In the 1970s, there was increasing participation in education and research. This decade saw the organization of dietetics into four major areas of practice—*diet therapy, education, community nutrition,* and *administration.* Interest in legislation also became important as the profession recognized the need for licensing of the dietetic practitioner.

EVALUATION AND CHANGE

The 1980s were a time of critical evaluation and change. The need for change brought about the emergence of specialties among nutrition professionals. Because of this, twenty-three Dietetic Practice Groups (DPGs) were established, each with its own standing rules, officers, newsletters, goals, and budget. As of 1998–99, the American Dietetic Association has twenty-nine current practice groups. (Checkout http://www.eatright.org on the Internet for more information.)

CURRENT PRACTICE GROUPS

Clinical Nutrition Management
Consultant Dietitians in Health Care Facilities
Diabetes Care and Education
Dietetic Educators of Practitioners
Dietetic Technicians in Practice
Dietetics in Developmental and Psychiatric Disorders
Dietetics in Physical Medicine and Rehabilitation
Dietitians in Business and Communications
Dietitians in General Clinical Practice

Dietitians in Nutrition Support
Environmental Nutrition
Food and Culinary Professionals
Gerontological Nutritionists
HIV/AIDS
Hunger and Malnutrition
Management in Food and Nutrition Systems
Nutrition Education for the Public
Nutrition Educators of Health Professionals
Nutrition Entrepreneurs
Nutrition in Complementary Care
Oncology Nutrition
Pediatric Nutrition
Perinatal Nutrition
Public Health Nutrition
Renal Dietitians
Research
School Nutrition Services
Sports, Cardiovascular, and Wellness Nutritionists
Vegetarian Nutrition

These practice groups provide American Dietetic Association members who have common interests and skills with a chance to share ideas and expand their expertise.

Now in the 1990s, nutritionists are focusing on the maintenance of general health versus just the treatment of disease. The objective is to help individuals obtain high-quality, tasty food and develop positive behaviors that will maintain and support health.

The American Dietetic Association, along with the practice of dietetics, has expanded into all areas—new food development and preparation, weight management, the treatment and prevention of disease, research, nutrition for sports, and many others. Because of this dynamic growth, there are almost unlimited opportunities in the field of nutrition. The time for the nutrition professional is *now!*

CHAPTER 3

DIETETIC EDUCATION

There are several education and experience routes that can be taken toward becoming a dietitian. The major education routes accredited or approved by the American Dietetic Association are Didactic Programs, Post-Baccalaureate Dietetic Internships, Coordinated Undergraduate Programs, and Preprofessional Practice Programs (AP4).

The Coordinated Undergraduate Programs and Dietetic Internships are accredited by the American Dietetic Association, Commission on Accreditation (Approval for Dietetics Education [CAADE]), in a process requiring site surveys. Programs in the other two pathways are approved by American Dietetic Association staff after a paper review; there is no formal accreditation of those programs.

Each of these approved education programs will be discussed in detail in this chapter.

FOUNDATION KNOWLEDGE AND SKILLS FOR DIDACTIC COMPONENT OF ENTRY-LEVEL DIETITIAN EDUCATION PROGRAMS[1]

Individuals interested in becoming Registered Dietitians (RDs) should expect to study a wide variety of topics focusing on food,

---

1. The American Dietetic Association, 1998–99 (http://www.eatright.org).

nutrition, and management. These areas are supported by the sciences: physical and biological, behavioral and social, and communication. Becoming a dietitian involves a combination of academic preparation, including a minimum of a baccalaureate degree, and a supervised practice component.

The following foundation knowledge and skill requirements are listed in the eight areas that students will focus on in the academic component of a dietetics program. Foundation learning is divided as follows: basic knowledge of a topic, working or in-depth knowledge of a topic as it applies to the profession of dietetics, and ability to demonstrate the skill at a level that can be developed further. To successfully achieve the foundation knowledge and skills, graduates must demonstrate the ability to communicate and collaborate, solve problems, and apply critical thinking skills.

These requirements may be met through separate courses, combined into one course, or as part of several courses as determined by the college or university sponsoring a program accredited or approved by the Commission on Accreditation/Approval for Dietetics Education (CAADE) of The American Dietetic Association.

Communications

Graduates will have *basic knowledge about:*
   Negotiation techniques
   Lay and technical writing
   Media presentations

Graduates will have *working knowledge of:*
   Interpersonal communication skills
   Counseling theory and methods
   Interviewing techniques
   Educational theory and techniques
   Concepts of human and group dynamics
   Public speaking
   Educational materials development

Graduates will have *demonstrated the ability to:*
    Present an educational session for a group
    Counsel individuals on nutrition
    Demonstrate a variety of documentation methods
    Explain a public policy position regarding dietetics
    Use current information technologies
    Work effectively as a team member

Physical and Biological Sciences

Graduates will have *basic knowledge about:*
    Exercise physiology

Graduates will have *working knowledge of:*
    Organic chemistry
    Biochemistry
    Physiology
    Microbiology
    Nutrient metabolism
    Pathophysiology related to nutrition care
    Fluid and electrolyte requirements
    Pharmacology: nutrient-nutrient and drug-nutrient interaction

Graduates will have *demonstrated the ability to:*
    Interpret medical terminology
    Interpret laboratory parameters relating to nutrition
    Apply microbiological and chemical considerations to process controls

Social Sciences

Graduates will have *basic knowledge about:*
    Public policy development

Graduates will have *working knowledge of:*
    Psychology
    Health behaviors and educational needs
    Economics and nutrition

Research

Graduates will have *basic knowledge about:*
  Research methodologies
  Needs assessments
  Outcomes-based research

Graduates will have *working knowledge of:*
  Scientific method
  Quality improvement methods

Graduates will have *demonstrated the ability to:*
  Interpret current research
  Interpret basic statistics

Food

Graduates will have *basic knowledge about:*
  Food technology
  Biotechnology
  Culinary techniques

Graduates will have *working knowledge of:*
  Sociocultural and ethnic food consumption issues and trends
    for various consumers
  Food safety and sanitation
  Food delivery systems
  Food and nonfood procurement
  Availability of nutrition programs in the community
  Formulation of local, state, and national food security policy
  Food production systems
  Environmental issues related to food
  Role of food in promotion of a healthy lifestyle
  Promotion of pleasurable eating
  Food and nutrition laws/regulations/policies
  Food availability and access for the individual, family, and
    community
  Applied sensory evaluation of food

Graduates will have *demonstrated the ability to:*
  Calculate and interpret nutrient composition of foods
  Translate nutrition needs into menus for individuals and groups
  Determine recipe/formula proportions and modifications for
    volume food production
  Write specifications for food and foodservice equipment
  Apply food science knowledge to functions of ingredients in
    food
  Demonstrate basic food preparation and presentation skills
  Modify recipe/formula for individual or group dietary needs

Nutrition

Graduates will have *basic knowledge about:*
  Alternative nutrition and herbal therapies
  Evolving methods of assessing health status

Graduates will have *working knowledge of:*
  Influence of age, growth, and normal development on nutri-
    tional requirements
  Nutrition and metabolism
  Assessment and treatment of nutritional health risks
  Medical nutrition therapy, including alternative feeding
    modalities, chronic diseases, dental health, mental health,
    and eating disorders
  Strategies to assess need for adaptive feeding techniques and
    equipment
  Health promotion and disease prevention theories and
    guidelines
  Influence of socioeconomic, cultural, and psychological fac-
    tors on food and nutrition behavior

Graduates will have *demonstrated the ability to:*
  Calculate and/or define diets for common conditions, i.e.,
    health conditions addressed by health promotion/disease
    prevention activities or chronic diseases of the general

population, e.g., hypertension, obesity, diabetes, diverticu-
lar disease
Screen individuals for nutritional risk
Collect pertinent information for comprehensive nutrition
assessments
Determine nutrient requirements across the lifespan, i.e.,
infants through geriatrics and a diversity of people, cul-
ture, and religions
Measure, calculate, and interpret body composition data
Calculate enteral and parenteral nutrition formulations

Management

Graduates will have *basic knowledge about:*
Program planning, monitoring, and evaluation
Strategic management
Facility management
Organizational change theory
Risk management

Graduates will have *working knowledge of:*
Management theories
Human resource management, including labor relations
Materials management
Financial management, including accounting principles
Quality improvement
Information management
Systems theory
Marketing theory and techniques
Diversity issues

Graduates will have *demonstrated the ability to:*
Determine costs of services/operation
Prepare a budget
Interpret financial data
Apply marketing principles

Health Care Systems

Graduates will have *basic knowledge about:*
Health care policy and administration
Health care delivery systems

Graduates will have *working knowledge of:*
Current reimbursement issues
Ethics of care

DIDACTIC PROGRAMS

These programs consist of a formalized baccalaureate degree offered at an accredited college or university and are approved by the American Dietetic Association.

The Didactic programs represent the current academic standards for the educational preparation of the professional dietitian. The actual academic requirements for completion of the program can be requested from the colleges and universities listed in Appendix B.

Graduates of Didactic programs who are verified by the program director may apply for dietetic internships or preprofessional practice programs to establish eligibility for active membership in the American Dietetic Association and/or to write the registration examination.

DIETETIC INTERNSHIP

The Dietetic Internship is a formalized post-baccalaureate educational program. It is sponsored and conducted by various organizations outside of educational institutions and is accredited by the ADA. Curriculums are designed to provide classroom and supervised clinical experiences to meet qualifications for dietetic practice. Students are required to enroll in an accredited internship following completion of the Diadactic program to qualify for taking the written registration examination.

Entrance into a Dietetic Internship is not guaranteed. The number of applicants is presently greater than the available positions. Therefore, it is important to be aware of the applicant selection processes.

The criteria for student selection used by most institutions include (*a*) academic record, which is the most heavily weighted; (*b*) letters of recommendation; and (*c*) student essays.

Academic Records

The grade point average (GPA) carries a relatively heavy weight. Educators view past academic success as a valid and reliable predictor of continued academic success. Success in an internship program depends upon a firm academic base. Among the relevant subject areas, science GPAs and English GPAs are considered good indicators of likelihood of success because of the strong emphasis on science and on written and oral communication skills in dietetics.

Letters of Recommendation

Letters of recommendation provide a means of learning about an individual's abilities in many areas. Most institutions usually request three letters, including character references from a professor in a major discipline, an academic advisor, a department chairperson, an instructor in a science course, or employers in professionally related jobs.

Student Essays

Student essays are used to gather information about an applicant's motivation, goals, and depth of interest in the profession.

Typical essays include professional goals, reasons for choosing dietetics as a profession, reasons for choosing the institution's internship program, and personal strengths and weaknesses.

An additional selection criterion is work experience. This ensures that the applicants have an understanding of the actual work performed and that they have a continuing interest in the profession. Volunteer work is as important as paid employment at this stage of the career.

Other selection variables include:

Conceptual Ability

Quality of written and oral expression, ability to master new information and skills, ability to understand complex new theories, and ability to translate theory into practice are all important considerations.

Overall Preparation

Relevance and quality of the applicant's previous educational experiences in school, in work, and in extracurricular activities; professionally related courses and electives taken as an undergraduate; refresher and/or advanced study done are also considered.

Self-Direction

Ability to set goals, organize one's own activities, and work independently are essential skills.

Leadership Ability

Formal recognition of leadership through election to office and honors and informal recognition by peers and others at school, work, and in extracurricular and community activities are indications of potential for success.

Ability to Perform Under Pressure

Flexibility, the ability to set priorities, the ability to set goals and organize work, physical stamina, and the ability to remain reasonably calm under stress are evaluated. The overall load carried by student during college (academic, work, and extracurricular family or community responsibilities) is considered.

Interpersonal Skills

Realistic self-confidence, the ability to sense the mood and concerns of others, appropriate use and interpretation of both verbal and nonverbal communications, the ability to adapt to a variety of people and situations, and concern for the well-being of others are also important.

COORDINATED UNDERGRADUATE PROGRAM

The Coordinated Undergraduate Program consists of four years of undergraduate study, with coordinated classroom and clinical experiences during the junior and senior years. Schools that offer the program (see Appendix C) must follow specific guidelines for program assessment, development, implementation, and evaluation. Each must also meet prescribed standards for organization and administration, faculty and staff, facilities, and student services.

In contrast to the Didactic program, the clinical component for the Coordinated Undergraduate Program is supervised by college or university faculty members and consists of a minimum of nine hundred hours. In the coordinated program, the need for an internship after graduation is eliminated. Thus, it takes five years to become professionally qualified in the Didactic program, but only four years in the this program.

PREPROFESSIONAL PRACTICE PROGRAMS (AP4)

The Preprofessional Practice Program provides a minimum of nine hundred hours of supervised practice. Programs follow completion of at least a baccalaureate degree and Didactic academic requirements. Some programs may be part-time, with supervised practice at a minimum of twenty hours per week and completed within a two-year period. This program replaces the six- to twelve-month work experience previously allowed (see Appendix E).

Each program is approved by the COE Division of Education Accreditation/Approval. All programs are in compliance with the Standards of Education. Program graduates who are verified by the program director are eligible to apply for active membership in the American Dietetic Association and/or to take the registration examination.

It is important to note that educational requirements in the field are under constant review and are subject to change. For the most up-to-date information, contact:

The American Dietetic Association
216 West Jackson Boulevard, Suite 800
Chicago, IL 60606-6995
(312) 899-0040
Fax: (312) 899-1979
http://www.eatright.org

A CHANGING CLIMATE

As dietetic leaders project the future education of dietitians, graduates of education programs must be prepared to perform the expected functions of the dietetic practitioner in a dramatically changing system. More than ever before, *education must be made relevant to practice.*

It is important for students to develop an education program that will meet their individual needs and practice interests. More specifically, the student should be aware of the areas in education that should be strengthened based on current practice demand. These include: a broader base, particularly in arts, humanities, and behavioral sciences; a greater emphasis on management and business; a greater emphasis on communications and networking; a greater emphasis on computer technology; a greater depth in scientific knowledge of nutrition; and a greater knowledge about food and cooking.

It is apparent that education must meet the individual's needs and specialty interests. Open course work should focus on those areas that the students perceive as being important to their practice in the field. In addition, students should seek volunteer work through hospitals, restaurants, resorts, outpatient facilities, nursing homes, etc. This will enable them to develop field experience to help determine realistic career objectives.

Dietitians of the future will not be able to serve as leaders unless the rigor and the credibility of their educational experiences are strengthened. The same is true for basic education programs, field experiences, advanced education in specialty areas, on-the-job training, graduate programs leading to advanced degrees, and continuing education.

CHAPTER 4

CLINICAL DIETETICS

The clinical dietitian is defined as a health care professional who has credentials as a Registered Dietitian and who affects the nutrition care of individuals and groups in health and illness. The clinical dietitian provides nutrition assessment and planning, implementation, and evaluation services; consults about foodservice systems; and manages departmental and personnel functions for nutrition care services. Clinical dietitians also coordinate patient care as a member of the health care team, maintain and update their individual skill and knowledge, and conduct applied research.

It is important to note also that the above responsibilities are not necessarily performed by *every* clinical dietitian in *every* position. What will be discussed in this chapter deals with the entry-level clinical dietitian. Subspecialties in clinical dietetics that require more specialized skills will be discussed later.

An entry-level position is defined as one that can be filled by a practitioner with experience of three years or less. The following is included to provide information about the skills necessary to perform as an entry-level clinical dietitian. According to the American Dietetic Association, the following responsibilities are those the entry-level clinical dietitian will be able to perform.

I. Plan and organize
   A. Use institutional and departmental standards to establish goals and priorities related to clinical nutrition, quality food, ethics, and education
   B. Participate in departmental program development using appropriate resources
      1. Compare budget and accounting systems to institutional standards
      2. Plan for computer utilization
      3. Develop guidelines for work schedules
      4. Develop policies and procedures
      5. Review evaluation strategies
      6. Assist with quality assurance planning
   C. Formulate an education plan
      1. Plan for personnel training
      2. Plan for nutritional and therapeutic needs of individuals and groups
      3. Select principles and theories of education appropriate for the desired plan
II. Gather and evaluate data
   A. Assess nutritional needs of individuals and groups
      1. Collect appropriate information for menu planning
      2. Collect appropriate information on the patient through the use of the medical record; questionnaires; interview; community agencies; anthropometric measurements; intakes of food, nutrients, and fluids; and use of drugs
      3. Establish methods for client inquiry (i.e., client or family interviews to obtain information in relation to physical, emotional, environmental, economic, and cultural factors
   B. Perform accurate dietary calculations and evaluate appropriate application

C. Demonstrate research techniques
   1. Review current literature
   2. Use resource materials effectively
   3. Identify problems, issues, priorities
   4. Select methodology for study
   5. Implement methodology
   6. Gather and evaluate data for use in improvement of program, system, or procedures
D. Appraise potential of individual for employment and upward mobility based on application and interview
E. Appraise employee for upward mobility based on performance evaluation
F. Evaluate products in relation to availability, cost, quality, and procurement
G. Evaluate nutritional programs and services of private or tax-supported agencies
H. Evaluate outcomes of patient education plan by assessing changes in food habits, teaching methods, and learner achievement
I. Contribute to and retrieve information from computer data storage

III. Communicate and report
   A. Delegate responsibility to personnel in nutrition care and foodservice systems
   B. Communicate through verbal and nonverbal means in interviewing, counseling, and evaluating
   C. Communicate in writing clearly, concisely, and in understandable terminology
   D. Communicate professional expertise in classes, meetings, conferences, and rounds
   E. Establish inter- and intradepartmental communication systems
   F. Conduct personnel training programs

G. Develop, update, and interpret policies and procedures

H. Monitor personnel utilization by evaluating workload of personnel and approving work schedules

IV. Counsel and supervise—Apply principles of psychology, principles of management, and counseling skills in the supervision and motivation of personnel and clients

A. Identify problem areas with personnel/clients

B. Assist personnel and clients to identify alternative solutions and implement changes

C. Review progress with personnel and clients

V. Apply scientific principles—Foodservice systems management

A. Establish standards for menu planning to coordinate with production and service

1. Approve regular and modified diet menus for nutrient adequacy, accuracy, and quality appropriate to individuals or groups

2. Evaluate menu cycle for changes

B. Monitor safety, security, and sanitation standards

C. Maintain budget controls

VI. Apply scientific principles—Clinical nutrition

A. Apply principles of management and nutrition to provide nutritional care for clients

1. Direct and evaluate personnel in the provision of nutritional care

2. Modify expenditures to comply with budget

3. Assess nutritional status and devise an individualized nutrition care plan

4. Implement plan through supervision of patient care and provision of nutrition education and follow-up to client and family

5. Evaluate and revise plan as necessary

B. Translate dietary modifications into menus
   1. Evaluate client acceptance of food
   2. Evaluate food quality, nutritional adequacy, and accuracy of dietary modification
   3. Approve regular and modified diet menus for nutrient adequacy, accuracy, and quality appropriate to individuals
   4. Evaluate dietary products and supplements
C. Monitor safety, security, and sanitation standards
D. Determine criteria for disease entities
   1. Document nutritional care of client according to established criteria
   2. Approve written documentation by dietetic technician
   3. Conduct audits of medical records at designated intervals
E. Utilize data for computer-assisted systems
   1. Menu planning and nutrient evaluation
   2. Calculation of client nutrient intake and utilization
   3. Client's medical database
   4. Criteria for audit
F. Apply current nutrition research for improvement of program or system

VII. Apply scientific principles in community nutrition—Apply principles of management and nutrition to provide nutritional care for clients in a program or agency
   A. Identify nutrition needs in the community
   B. Assess community resources

VIII. Demonstrate creativity
   A. Apply creative and innovative methods and ideas
      1. Solve problems
      2. Merchandise products, services, nutrition, and the profession

3. Plan nutrition and foodservice programs
4. Develop educational methods and teaching aids

B. Apply scientific principles using innovative methods in foodservice management, clinical nutrition, and community nutrition

C. Continue to seek new ways of communicating with others

IX. Exhibit professional performance and accountability

A. Maintain registration as a professional dietitian

B. Practice American Dietetic Association Code of Professional Practice and Guidelines for Professional Conduct

C. Maintain a professional standard of practice

D. Maintain current professional knowledge by reviewing the literature, maintaining updated resource files, participating in institutional and professional conferences and seminars, and writing technical reports, critical reviews, and articles

E. Utilize problem-solving methods

F. Practice self-assessment and assessment of others by developing goals for improvement

G. Integrate self into the professional role by applying interpersonal skills and assuming leadership roles in the profession

H. Integrate own position and role into a program or system

I. Promote departmental and program objectives

J. Provide continuing education for staff and personal development based on needs

K. Determine legal implications in the practice of dietetics and seek appropriate liability coverage

L. Follow institutional policies for the protection of personnel and clients

M. Seek information on current legislation affecting personnel, patient care, and the profession

N. Comply with employer and institutional contracts, and government regulations

These skills represent performance at an entry level, showing depth of knowledge acquired, but they do not indicate that all practitioners will utilize all skills.

CHAPTER 5

CLINICAL DIETETICS— SUBSPECIALTIES

The field of dietetics is becoming very specialized, as is the case in the field of medicine, where physicians often choose to specialize in one area. The clinical dietitian today is expanding her or his skills in the development of a speciality, and many are becoming nutrition experts in highly developed areas.

In this chapter we will discuss the various segments of clinical dietetics: research, pediatrics, critical care, renal dietetics, diabetes, and sports and cardiovascular nutrition. These subspecialties broaden the scope of clinical dietetic practice and provide interested individuals an opportunity to become expert in a particular area.

RESEARCH

Dietitians become specialized in the area of research through their work in clinical research centers and through public health projects. Most start out in general clinical practice and then go on to research, for which a master of science degree is usually required. The research environment may be in a university, a hospital (inpatient and/or outpatient setting), or a public health setting.

Candidates interested in research work need to be careful, objective, and self-starters with clinical experience. Additional training may include the areas of grant writing to acquire money, scientific journal writing, and statistics.

Positive aspects of choosing a career in this area include the ability to work independently and with other high-level professionals. Activity in research also demands the development of knowledge of many aspects of nutrition; e.g., biochemical, physiological, and psychological.

With substantial research training and experience, a Registered Dietitian can move from one area to another to do research, rather than staying in one specialization area.

The future direction of research will probably focus on the effectiveness of nutritional intervention, as society focuses on the importance of preventive measures in terms of both cost and health effectiveness. Although the exact nature of the link between nutrition factors and health remains controversial, there appears to be a broad consensus that diet, nutrition, and eating habits are significantly related to health status. These health issues will expand the opportunities available to the research dietitian.

PEDIATRICS

Dietitians enter pediatric practice because of the opportunity to work with children. Becoming specialized in pediatrics requires practice in a children's hospital or a hospital with a pediatric unit, or may require an advanced degree specializing in infant/child nutrition. Work settings vary, but usually the practitioner begins in a general hospital pediatric environment and then moves on to do other pediatric work. These environments may include medical centers, hospitals, schools, day-care centers, physician offices, and research centers.

Training for entry-level positions in pediatric practice includes registration with one to two years of experience in the subspecialty area.

The demand for pediatric practitioners will be influenced by the birth rate, expanding child care programs, legislative trends, and technology. Another area that will impact pediatric practice will be the expanded focus on maternal nutrition to improve the outcome of pregnancy. This area may extend the pediatric practitioner's involvement to include maternal and prenatal care.

CRITICAL CARE

Dietitians in critical care have a strong therapeutic background, typically working in a university or teaching hospital providing care to the critically ill patient. Most have obtained a master's degree or advanced training beyond the clinical internship. Positive features of this specialty include increased contact with medical staff and opportunities for research, teaching, and publishing.

Critical care dietitians work with parenteral and enteral nutrition, nutritional assessments, and drug–nutrient interactions. They also work closely with patients to improve nutritional status.

Subspecialties in this area are increasing due to the importance of nutrition in critical illness and the specifics of nutrition therapy. These subspecialties include nutrition support services, oncology, hematology, neonatology, and advanced burn care.

These specialties involve high-pressure work environments and long hours that demand leadership, assertiveness, and career commitment from the dietetic professional.

RENAL DIETITIANS

Renal dietetics deals with nutrition therapy for those individuals with kidney problems. Training for this specialty area requires clinical experience with advanced training, usually on a renal unit in a hospital or dialysis center.

Registered dietitians interested in practicing in this area require special traits to handle intense, long-term patient care, including the patients' psychological and sociological needs. They must be dedicated and have an interest in maintaining current educational status. Rapid changes in knowledge in this area necessitate constant continuing education.

Major work activities of renal dietitians include patient and family education, development of teaching materials, participation in medical rounds, interpretation of laboratory tests, and nutrition education of allied professionals. These responsibilities require knowledge about food composition, drug-nutrient interaction, and fluid electrolyte management in the body.

DIABETES CARE

Dietitians specializing in diabetes care and education usually work in outpatient facilities or inpatient programs provided by hospitals. The required education includes a bachelor of science degree with registration status. Additional course work or a master's degree is not required but is helpful due to the complexity of the disease.

Diabetes care requires long-term treatment and patient education. This provides the dietitian with an opportunity to develop individualized long-term care and to follow the patient and family for an extended time. The dietitian will develop nutrition care plans and educate the client regarding nutrition, psychosocial problems, and exercise. Diabetes care also enables the dietitian to work as a team member.

Opportunities in this area will probably expand due to the increased incidence and increasing knowledge of the disease. Also, technology will continue to shape this area of practice, as research and computers continue to affect methods of treatment.

SPORTS AND CARDIOVASCULAR DIETITIANS

Sports and cardiovascular dietitians usually begin with a clinical background as a registered dietitian and then obtain a master of science degree in nutrition and exercise physiology. YMCAs, schools, universities, and businesses all provide a variety of opportunities to practice. This area will see the greatest expansion in the future, due to the increased awareness of business, industry, and the general public about the importance of nutrition and exercise.

Candidates are drawn to this area because of a personal interest in sports and because clients are actively seeking nutrition information. Work activities include individual diet/nutrition counseling, development of education materials and audiovisual aids, computer nutrient analysis, writing, and research.

As more is learned about the combined importance of nutrition and exercise, the demand for dietitians in this area will increase and their work environments will expand to include hospitals, the community, and specialty work in professional and amateur athletics.

CONCLUSION

Many of these clinical subspecialties require advanced training after registration, which includes a master of science or Ph.D. degree, and significant work experience within the specialty area. This trend will continue as research and technology expand the "science" of dietetics and nutrition. Also, dietitians will do more independent research, develop policies and procedures, and consult and teach individuals and groups.

CHAPTER 6

COMMUNITY DIETETICS

The dietitian in a community setting plays an important role as a member of the health care team. The community dietitian "counsels individuals and groups on nutritional practices designed to prevent disease and promote good health. Working in such places as public health clinics, home health agencies, and health maintenance organizations, they evaluate individual needs, develop nutritional care plans, and instruct individuals and their families. Dietitians working in home health agencies may provide instruction on grocery shopping and food preparation to the elderly, or patients with AIDS, cancer, or diabetes."[1]

Areas of subspecialty in community nutrition include home health care, health maintenance organizations (HMOs), private practice, and business and industry.

HOME HEALTH CARE

The community dietitian will often provide nutrition services to clients in their homes. Usually a referral is made from a hospital health team to the dietitian. The dietitian reviews the patient's

---

1. *Occupational Outlook Handbook.* Washington: U.S. Department of Labor, 1998–99, 193.

medical record, takes dietary history, assesses the patient's nutritional status, records food likes and dislikes, and develops a nutritional care plan based on pertinent information contributing to nutritional care. The nutrition care plan will then help determine what services the dietitian will provide. These services may include assessment of dietary intake by computer nutrient analysis; consultation with physicians prescribing diets; client and family counseling; follow-up conferences and in-service education with nurses, therapists, and home health aides; and the recording, reporting, and monitoring of progress and results of nutritional care.

Once developed, the plan is then discussed with the client or home sponsor for the client. Issues that may arise in relation to home care may include weight gain from overeating, lack of exercise, and complications in medical conditions. It is important to maintain contact with other health team members, and the community dietitian may need to expand the care plan as the case proceeds.

The dietitian, by maintaining contact with the other health care providers, can identify specific problems and refer them to the team member responsible for that area of specialization. In addition, "mini" home nutrition courses that focus on different areas of nutrition can be provided. The dietitian may provide sample menus for normal and modified diets, depending on the client's lifestyle and medical therapy. The dietitian, therefore, needs to be aware of food costs, who purchases the food, cultural food preferences, and food preparation facilities. In this way, home visits provide an opportunity for the dietitian to identify socioeconomic problems and then to determine instructional techniques to use in gaining acceptance and adherence to the diet and nutrition care plan.

Although not all clients need nutrition services provided in the home, many clients do need the assistance of a dietitian, including:

1. Those whose diets need modification
2. Those whose conditions don't improve because of an improper diet

3. Those whose food plans are prescribed as part of the over-all treatment of their conditions
4. Those who need to be monitored, i.e., mal- or undernour-ished patients
5. Those who need dietary counseling but are unable to travel
6. Those who need follow-up after discharge from a hospital/nursing home

The career benefits of providing home health care nutrition ser-vices are many. Home health care provides the ability to develop a long-term care plan for the client and to provide continued follow-up. The dietitian performs independently and also as a team mem-ber, and is responsible for the development of educational materi-als for client use.

In addition, the dietitian, by providing home health services, may reduce the total cost of health care. Examples of potential cost savings are:

1. Reducing need for rehospitalization because of malnutri-tion, uncontrolled diabetes, and other conditions
2. Preventing fractures due to disorientation or weakness related to malnutrition
3. Delaying kidney dialysis treatment
4. Preventing food poisoning from improper food sanitation at home
5. Permitting earlier discharge of patients with parenteral or enteral feedings
6. Assisting the patient to understand and use new technolo-gies, thus preventing or delaying reinstitutionalization
7. Hastening healing of postoperative patients
8. Using a trained professional who is more efficient and accurate in the adjustment and readjustment of individual-ized diets

Educational requirements include entry-level status and two to three years experience in a clinical setting. An advanced degree (M.S.) is preferred.

HEALTH MAINTENANCE ORGANIZATIONS

Health maintenance organizations (HMOs) are comprehensive medical facilities where, through an employer, families and/or individuals prepay for health care. HMOs were developed to restructure health care delivery systems to provide equitable, high-quality care for all; provide optimal utilization of health personnel; control costs; and satisfy consumers. They are designed to bring together health services that individuals and families are most likely to need for a fixed premium paid in advance by subscribers. An HMO is dedicated to providing comprehensive care, defined as a full range of health services with emphasis on prevention; care continuity, coordinated on a family basis, throughout each member's life cycle and health–sickness cycle; and care that is organized and carried out to give maximum health care service for the consumer dollars.

The basic principle by which HMO operations will be successful lies in keeping people well, in order to avoid the more complex and costly services needed to treat illness and return people to health. In this way, the HMO provides a medical setting outside the hospital where a dietitian can develop a varied practice and become more involved with each client by providing follow-up care.

Dietitians in this area are diet counselors, health educators, and program evaluators. The dietitian deals with both individuals and families, as well as with the health care team, to provide total health services. In the role of diet counselor, the dietitian provides diet therapy to diabetics, cardiovascular patients, and hypertensives, and diet therapy during and following pregnancy. As the health educator, the dietitian teaches self-care, using nutrition as a framework to build positive behavior patterns. The dietitian may also be involved in specialty clinics to deal with obesity, alcoholism, smoking cessation, and weight reduction. As a program evaluator, the dietitian has the opportunity to work with HMO administrators to initiate new and evaluate ongoing programs.

Nutrition services in an HMO, as suggested by the American Dietetic Association, may be as follows:

Phase of HMO Operation	Nutritional Care Goal	Nutritional Care Activities[2]
Health appraisal and referral	To identify potential problems and plan for continuing surveillance or appropriate care	Assessment of food practices and nutritional status. Referral for corroboration. Data input into patient information systems.
Environmental protection and disease prevention; health maintenance	To prepare patients and their families to assume responsibility for their own care and to manage early symptoms to prevent complications	Individual counseling. Group teaching. Development and/or evaluation of nutri-methods and materials. Training and continuing education for medical, dental, and other professional staff; technical consultation. Training and continuing education for dietetic supportive personnel. Referral to, and liaison with, food assistance and other nutrition-related community programs. Leadership in seeking solutions to community-wide nutrition problems. Consultation to group care facilities.

2. The American Dietetic Association Position Paper on Nutrition Services in Health Maintenance Organizations. *J. Am. Diet. Assoc.*

Phase of HMO Operation	Nutritional Care Goal	Nutritional Care Activities[2]
Acute and intensive care	To develop and implement immediate and long-range individualized nutritional care plans for in- or outpatients	Most of the activities described above. Ongoing participation in health team planning, direct nutritional assessment and counseling, and evaluation. Planning appropriate group food service. Health team staff conferences. Initial and follow-up counseling in regard to normal and therapeutic nutritional needs. Input into clinical records.
Restoration and extended care	To assist patients and their families with long-term health problems to attain and maintain adequate diets	Most of the activities described above. Assistance in adjusting home environment to maximize independent functioning in activities in and outside the home. Liaison with noncontact services or programs helpful in carrying out the nutritional care plan.

Nutritional care activities clearly will overlap and seldom will be restricted to a single phase of operation.

The education required of the dietitian is a baccalaureate degree with registration credentials; a master's degree is suggested. The training in research and analysis that a master's degree–level person has provides the dietitian with more credibility and an increased opportunity for input into planning programs at the HMO.

Also helpful is knowledge of, and experience in, community organization and community health services and resources in order to provide counseling and direction in planning and implementing nutritional care. The dietitian should also be capable of training and supervising dietetic personnel and coordinating nutrition programs with other health care services.

Job satisfaction in this area is high because dietitians are occupying positions where they are gaining respect, credibility, and public confidence. However, the R.D. must become more visible to other health care personnel and must be able to "sell nutrition" and explain why it is important that he or she become part of the medical/health care team.

PRIVATE PRACTICE

Consultant dietitians work under contract with health care facilities or in their own private practices. They perform nutrition screening for their clients and offer advice on diet-related concerns such as weight loss or cholesterol reduction. Some work for wellness programs, sports teams, supermarkets, and other nutrition-related businesses. They may consult with foodservice managers, providing expertise in sanitation, safety procedures, budgeting, and planning.[3]

According to the ADA, the following are suggested roles the consulting dietitian performs:

    I. Services provided to businesses or groups

        A. Evaluates and monitors foodservice systems, making recommendations to provide nutritionally adequate food

        B. Develops budget proposals and recommends procedures for cost controls

        C. Plans, organizes, and conducts orientation and in-service educational programs for foodservice personnel

---

3. *Occupational Outlook Handbook* (1998–99 edition), p. 193.

    D. Plans layout design and determines equipment requirements for foodservice facilities

    E. Recommends and monitors standards for sanitation, safety, and security in foodservice

    F. Develops menu patterns

    G. Develops, maintains, and uses pertinent record systems related to the needs of the organization and the consultant dietitian

    H. Provides guidance and evaluation of the job performance of dietetic personnel

    I. Maintains effective verbal and written communications and public relations, inter- and intradepartmentally

II. Services provided to individuals

    A. Assesses, develops, implements, and evaluates nutritional care plans and provides for follow-up, including written reports

    B. Consults with and counsels clients regarding selection and procurement of food to meet optimal nutrition

    C. Develops menu patterns

    D. Develops, uses, and evaluates educational materials related to services provided

    E. Consults with the health care team concerning the nutritional care of clients

    F. Interprets, evaluates, and utilizes current research relating to nutritional care

Education and experience necessary to practice as a consultant dietitian include:

    1. Registration (R.D.)

    2. One to four years of clinical or community nutrition experience

A master's degree in business and/or nutritional sciences is not required but is suggested.

The dietitian in private practice will carry over into career areas already discussed and those to follow. These areas provide population groups where consultant dietitians can market their services.

As an example, a consultant might become involved in the employee health service of a corporation. For economic reasons, corporations are focusing on preventive health care and education to decrease health care costs and increase worker productivity. By changing the employee's "health profile," a corporation can save money by cutting sick time, decreasing the use of medical care, and avoiding early retirement due to disablement.

Other areas for development of a private practice include:

- Physician's office or physician's group
- Nursing homes/hospices
- Psychologists' groups
- Dental offices
- Weight-loss clinics
- Sports facilities
- Spas

To facilitate practice in these areas as well as others, the dietitian must determine: the nutrition needs and interests of clients; the format of counseling sessions; how to promote the service; how to build a client base; additional resources available for clients; the competition; and fees.

Actual services provided may include:

1. Weight reduction, weight maintenance, or weight gain nutrition counseling
2. Nutrition education
3. Obesity, diabetes, cardiovascular disease treatment
4. Bulimia/anorexia counseling
5. Premenstrual syndrome therapy
6. Smoking cessation counseling and therapy
7. Substance abuse nutrition therapy
8. Publishing for newspapers and magazines

The positive aspects of a career as a consultant include the ability to sell oneself, developing an assertive, business profile; respect as a health professional from the medical community and also the public; and the challenge to succeed on your own. Some drawbacks may be the financial risk and often having to rely on physician referral for patients. Also, payment for services may not be insurance-reimbursable. In addition, the general public may lack the knowledge to understand exactly what the dietitian can provide.

Although there are obstacles as a consultant, the highly self-motivated dietitian can develop a successful and rewarding independent practice. This community subspecialty will continue to expand as the general public becomes more aware of dietetic services and the importance of nutrition in maintaining health.

BUSINESS AND INDUSTRY

Business and industry may be considered the area with the most rapid growth for dietitians. In the past, dietitians in business and industry typically worked for food companies developing new food products. Now, as "health" becomes a prominent focus in the private sector, opportunities for the dietitian seem limitless.

Industry recruiters, as well as executives in foodservice management companies, report a continual need for dietitians in this area, especially those with management skills. Many businesses hire dietitians for their technical expertise, providing the company with a competitive edge in marketing their products and services. Also, public relations firms are hiring dietitians to help them provide nutrition information to their clients.

To take advantage of the opportunities available, dietitians need to expand their skills to include: management training, especially finance and marketing; oral, written, and media communication skills; and the ability to "sell" oneself to promote ideas and new projects and to improve the image of the profession.

Recruiters and employers in this area are looking for the dietitian profile that projects:

- Self-confidence in professional knowledge and ability to learn new information
- An enthusiastic attitude about the job and about working
- Achievement orientation
- Assertive behavior in promotion of self, ideas, and products or services of employing corporation
- Willingness to travel or relocate
- Good communication skills
- Willingness to work long hours to accomplish a job
- Ability to utilize criticism for personal and professional growth
- Interest in upgrading and developing skills for advancement through a variety of continuing education programs

The education required for an entry-level position in business and industry includes a B.S. from an approved dietetic program, registration, and management course work. Management experience is valuable but not necessary in all cases. Also, course work in accounting and personnel management is suggested. For the dietitian wanting to move into a middle or top management position, a master's degree in business administration (M.B.A.) is becoming necessary.

Specific skills and knowledge required when entering business and industry include finance, writing and communication skills, marketing, public speaking, computer efficiency, personnel management, budgeting and accounting, economics, food sciences, long-range planning and time management, and cost containment.

Types of positions available to the dietitian interested in practicing in business and industry include:

- Advertising, public relations, and marketing
- Anthropology research

- Architects or consultants to materials managers
- Chemical laboratory representatives
- Computer software development and sales
- Consumer affairs
- Cooking school instruction
- Equipment companies—service and sales
- Fitness and wellness centers, resorts, and spas
- Food brokers and distributors
- Hospital administration and management
- Lawyers involved with nutrition regulations, codes, and labor
- Nursing
- Personnel directors
- Pharmaceutical companies—sales, product development, marketing
- Product development—food and equipment
- Production manager
- Restaurant management
- Retail stores—food demonstration and cookware sales
- Social/nutrition programs—development, evaluation, and management

Specific subspecialty areas in this field are emphasized in the following sections.

Food Product Companies

In food product companies dietitians are hired to serve as advisory staff to corporate management on nutrition-related issues in product development, labeling, advertising, legislation, public relations, marketing, and consumer education. Skills necessary beyond technical expertise include skills in human relations, the desire to excel, flexibility, and good oral and written communications skills.

Sales Companies

Sales companies utilize dietitians for their technical expertise regarding diet modification and food production and distribution. Dietitians have excellent opportunities as sales representatives because of their familiarity with the food and medicine industry. They have knowledge about medical therapy, know the language, and, therefore, can use a "soft-sell" approach. Additional skills required beyond technical expertise include skills in marketing, accounting, financial analysis, labor relations, and economics.

Fitness and Wellness Centers

Fitness and wellness centers, resorts, and spas utilize dietitians for their menu planning and diet modification skills, as well as client nutrition education and writing for popular press, newsletters, and educational material development. This area requires additional knowledge in marketing, finance, public relations, writing, and accounting, and a well-rounded nutrition background that focuses on health maintenance.

CONCLUSION

Community dietitians increasingly will be challenged to demonstrate specialized competencies and meet the total needs of the community. However, due to the unique role the dietitian may play as a health team member, opportunities will continue to expand—the future in community dietetics is bright.

CHAPTER 7

THE ADMINISTRATIVE DIETITIAN: FOODSERVICE SYSTEMS MANAGEMENT

Many nutrition professionals are entering the field of foodservice systems management. Here, there is a need for the administrative dietitian, a management specialist. This area of dietetic practice includes many administrative and management responsibilities. Although this area may not sound dynamic, it has opportunities available for management growth, long-term job security and benefits, and the ability to develop experience that can be applied in other fields.

Management is the major function of the administrative dietitian, specifically, foodservice systems management. This area of management is defined as the process of accomplishing foodservice system objectives. These include menu planning, food procurement, production, distribution, and service.

PROFESSIONAL ROLES

The roles performed by the entry-level dietitian in foodservice systems management are delineated in the following list. These represent a combination of actual roles, which currently exist, and those that ought to exist. These roles are abstracted from a role delineation study for Foodservice Systems Management published by the American Dietetic Association.

The foodservice systems management professional performs the following roles:

1. Focuses foodservice operations on nutrition goals of a target market
2. Advances practitioner competence through self-improvement programs
3. Promotes positive working relationships with others whose work has an impact on foodservice systems
4. Utilizes current foodservice systems and nutrition information in management and research
5. Manages foodservice subsystems, including food procurement, production, distribution, and service
6. Manages foodservice system resources, including human, material, physical, and operational assets
7. Manages quality assurance programs in area of responsibility
8. Advocates action that advances foodservice systems management and improves nutrition status of consumers

EDUCATION

The education required includes entry-level qualifications with three or fewer years of experience. Specific areas of study include:

- Principles of food systems management: provides an overall view of the management of food systems, including personnel involved in food preparation and service; equipment for operation; the purchasing of food and supplies; and the management of time and money.
- Quantity food purchasing and preparation: provides in-depth experience in menu planning, food preparation techniques, and cooking procedures to ensure quality food production.

- Development, utilization, and maintenance of physical resources: provides education in planning a foodservice facility,
with exposure to equipment salespeople, consultants, engi-
neers, and architects in developing the layout plan. Learns
how to write equipment specifications and prepare cost esti-
mates. Also learns equipment operation, sanitation, and preventive maintenance guidelines.
- Operations analysis: knowledge is gained in computer pro-
gramming for use as a decision-making tool in foodservice
for cost containment, food purchasing, stock maintenance,
and as a carryover into clinical dietetics for modified diet
menu planning and preparation.

CAREER CONSIDERATIONS

Job satisfaction is high when the administrative dietitian is able to
assume several roles. These include: a middle-management role as
the director of a foodservice system; an advisor role to top-level
administrators of the organization; and as a personnel administrator
of other dietitians, foodservice employees, and dietetic students.

Barriers to career development and expansion in this area
include: lack of visibility; the perception that dietitians, in general,
lack adequate management skills; and the actual shortage of dietitians willing to assume management positions, which causes hospital and other administrators to look elsewhere to hire
administrative personnel.

CONCLUSION

Current and future technology will aid in the development of
new administrative roles and challenges. The administrative dieti-

tian must be willing to sacrifice traditional approaches and adopt new methods to deal with cost containment, while maintaining quality foodservice, increased productivity, and an increase in food and clinical nutrition services. To meet these challenges, the administrative dietitian must be assertive, knowledgeable, willing to work long and hard hours, and goals-oriented.

CHAPTER 8

OTHER HEALTH PROFESSIONALS AND THE DIETITIAN

A *profession* is defined as "a calling requiring specialized knowledge and often long and intensive academic preparation."[1] A *professional* "conforms to the technical or ethical standards of the profession...exhibiting a courteous, conscientious, and generally businesslike manner in the workplace."[2] As a professional, the dietitian may interact with other professionals in order to provide the best care possible to the client. The team members may include a physician, pharmacist, exercise physiologist, nurse, psychologist, and others. The potential role of each will be discussed here.

One example of a team practice environment would concern the treatment of obesity. Obesity therapy requires psychological, medical, physical fitness, and dietary management. The concept of the team approach is imperative for the successful treatment of this problem and others. In this approach, the dietitian, as the primary care provider, may be responsible for medical monitoring, behavioral and cognitive counseling, and nutrition education. The dietitian may also be responsible for the patient's total care and

---

1. *Webster's Tenth New Collegiate Dictionary,* 1996, p. 930.
2. Ibid.

may act as the coordinator of all team efforts. In this example, the dietitian requires medical and psychological training, as well as traditional dietetic experience.

The medical role of the dietitian may be to take blood pressure, weigh the patient weekly, and order appropriate lab tests. As she or he monitors these aspects, problems can be related to the physician to ensure complete medical care. The dietitian may also arrange an appointment with an exercise physiologist for a fitness evaluation and initiate an exercise program.

It is important for the dietitian to develop a relationship with the patient so that personal problems can be discussed. Basic counseling techniques may be used to help patients to better understand their behavior. The dietitian may also be qualified to identify more serious psychological problems and refer the patient to a psychologist or psychiatrist in the community.

This example of the team concept depicts how the dietitian may work closely with allied health professionals to provide total care to the patient. Other ways in which the dietitian may interact with allied health professionals include:

- Consultation with a pharmacist to discuss drug-nutrient interaction, vitamin/mineral supplementation, or parenteral/enteral product use
- Interaction with a nurse to attain information regarding actual patient progress and home health care problems

As a professional working with other health team members, the dietitian must be confident, knowledgeable, and able to apply all acquired skills to provide treatment to patients and to effectively communicate with other professionals.

CHAPTER 9

SALARIES AND JOB SATISFACTION

SALARIES

It is important to realize that salary levels for dietitians vary greatly. Some of the variables affecting salary range include practice specialty, area of the nation, size of the city, length of employment, experience, practice environment, the number of qualified professionals in the area, and the cost of living. National salary comparisons are scarce. The American Dietetic Association in 1997[1] reported the median salary ranges for full-time (thirty-one or more hours per week), registered dietitians as:

Practice Area	Salary
Clinical nutrition	$35,491
Food and nutrition management	44,924
Community nutrition	38,870
Consultation and business	46,040
Education and research	45,211

---

1. Bryk, Joseph A. and Tami Kornblum Soto. Report on the 1997 Membership Database of The American Dietetic Association. *J. Am. Diet. Assoc.* 99: 107, 1999.

In 1997, the estimated median annual incomes for dietetic technicians for the two most common areas of practice were: clinical nutrition, $24,219, and food and nutrition management, $28,576. (Salary levels may vary with geographical location, scope of responsibility, and number of applicants.)

ADDITIONAL BENEFITS

Other areas of compensation that should be valued when considering positions are employee benefits. These benefits are a valuable asset to the nutrition professional. These additional benefits may include:

A. Disability benefits, sick and mental health leave; insurance— group life, accident, hospitalization; other
   1. Twelve-day sick leave per year
   2. Group life insurance equal to annual salary; hospitalization and medical insurance
   3. Dental insurance
   4. Discounts on goods and services purchased from company
   5. Employee meals
   6. Profit sharing
   7. Special bonuses
B. Vacation and holidays
C. Plan for salary increments and opportunities for advancement
D. Retirement plans
E. Professional growth, e.g., attendance at professional meetings, education, sabbaticals
F. Travel allowances
G. Employee fitness program and facility

As a prospective nutrition professional, it is important to check with area practice groups about current salaries and benefits.

Another resource is the classified ad section of the journal of the American Dietetic Association. This section will provide regional salaries for current openings in the field and the qualifications necessary.

JOB SATISFACTION

In today's ever-expanding and changing job market, it is becoming more important to choose a career that will provide stimulation and rewards. Nutrition is definitely one of these career choices.

There are multiple aspects of a job that lead to job satisfaction. These considerations include interest in the work, goals that are reasonable, work that is mentally challenging and not too physically demanding, tasks that can be successfully completed, acknowledgment of work well done, a cooperative environment, and work that builds self-esteem.

Finally, it is important for the nutrition professional to evaluate all aspects of the potential job to determine if the employer can provide the satisfying work environment and work experience for the development of a rewarding career. The time has come when it is the professionals' responsibility to determine whether they are right for the job and whether they can enthusiastically tackle the job expectations to achieve job satisfaction.

CHAPTER 10

A SUPPORTIVE NUTRITION POSITION—THE DIETETIC TECHNICIAN

It is generally recognized that dietitians need assistance in performing their professional responsibilities. Dietetic technicians are technically skilled individuals who have been prepared to assume a supportive nutrition role and work under the guidance of a registered dietitian.

The registered dietitian oversees the assessment, planning, and evaluation of individual patients, with a dietetic technician assisting in any or all phases of the nutrition care process. The dietetic technician has responsibilities in assigned areas of nutrition care, such as dietary instruction of selected individuals, consultation with the health team, and monitoring of patient food quality and acceptance.

The American Dietetic Association recognizes these roles as appropriate for the dietetic technician who has completed an approved associate degree program.

At the client level, the clinical dietetic technician assists the registered dietitian in clinical practice to provide direct nutrition services to patients. The technician is responsible for:

1. Using predetermined criteria in screening patients to identify those at nutritional risk and collecting data for use in assessing dietary status

2. Following guidelines established by the registered dietitian to develop nutrition care plans for individual patients
3. Providing technical services in the implementation of nutrition care plans
4. Monitoring the effect of nutrition intervention and assessing patient food acceptance
5. Providing diet counseling and education to individuals not at nutritional risk

Within the second level, "intraprofessional" relationships, the dietetic technician cooperates with the clinical dietitian in promoting standards of practice and using current knowledge to solve nutrition problems of individual patients.

At the third or "interprofessional" level, the technician is responsible for coordinating the nutrition care of assigned patients with other health services and coordinating designated nutrition care plans with institutional foodservice activities.

At the "intra-organizational" level, the dietetic technician utilizes established standards and procedures to implement the system of patient nutrition care. This responsibility includes:

1. Utilizing established procedures for making available designated special food products and dietary supplements
2. Supervising diet clerks and other patient foodservice personnel
3. Developing and implementing a program of orientation, training, and in-service education for patient foodservice personnel

Employment environments for the dietetic technician include community hospitals, intermediate or skilled nursing facilities, and university medical centers. This indicates that health care is the primary employment outlet.

Like the registered dietitian specializing in specific areas, the dietetic technician is expanding into subspecialty areas. These subspecialties may include work in:

- Clinical psychiatric areas
- Pediatric practice
- Critical care
- Foodservice management
- Community programs
- Wellness centers
- Business and industry

EDUCATION

The dietetic technician is a professional who holds an associate of arts degree and has completed 450 hours of supervised experience in the area of either nutrition care or foodservice management. The technician is viewed as the assistant to the clinical dietitian or the public health nutritionist. The approved program of dietetic technician education prepares the technician to conduct patient interviews; to assist patients in the daily choice of a balanced diet; to give routine dietary instructions; to arrange meal plans for modified diets; to assist patients in health care institutions or clients in the community in meal planning and food purchasing for the entire family; and to assist the dietitian or nutritionist in preparing educational materials for various teaching programs.

The table that follows represents the recommended American Dietetic Association pattern for an approved program of dietetic technician education leading to competency in nutrition care.

Sample Dietetic Technician Nutrition Care Program

Course	Semester Hours
Semester 1	
Nutrition Care I	3
Supervised Field Experience	1
Foods	3
Health Field	1
Contemporary Sociology	3
Open Course	3
Open Course	3
Total	17
Semester 2	
Nutrition Care II	3
Supervised Field Experience	2
Education	3
Health Field	1
Open Course	3
Open Course	3
Total	15
Semester 3	
Nutrition Care III	3
Supervised Field Experience	3
Health Care Delivery Systems	3
Management	3
Open Course	3
Total	15
Semester 4	
Nutrition Care IV	3
Supervised Field Experience	4
Dietetic Seminar	1
Open Course	3
Open Course	3
Open Course	3
Total	17

In *Nutrition Care I,* students study normal nutrition. This course covers why and how people eat; what influences malnutrition; how to bring about changes in food habits; cultural food patterns; the nature of food and its work in the body; the normal process of digestion, absorption, and metabolism; nutrients and their functions; nutrition in the life cycle; and food fads.

Nutrition Care II covers the study of diet therapy. This course is concerned with the nutritional care of the patient who has problems of the upper gastrointestinal region and progresses to nutritional care of patients with congestive heart failure, hypertension, atherosclerosis, hyperlipoproteinemea, obesity, and diabetes.

Nutrition Care III involves study of the general problems of nutritional care of patients with problems of digestion, absorption, and metabolism and fluid and electrolyte balance.

Nutrition Care IV emphasizes community nutrition learning to deal with inborn errors of metabolism, anemias, arthritis, and more.

The *Foods* course considers an overview of foods; the basic four food groups; principles of menu planning and food purchasing for the home, including budgeting; food stamps; and interpretation of food advertising and labels. It also covers food additives, food sanitation and spoilage, unit pricing, and FDA rulings.

Dietetic Seminar introduces the health field and the roles of practitioners in dietetics. The student is also introduced to various feeding systems and the team efforts to provide adequate nutrition care.

THE FUTURE

The future of employment as a dietetic technician is expanding as the increased utilization of the technician by various organizations will lead to cost containment, better use of supportive personnel, reduction in staffing needs, and functioning of dietitians at the level of proficiency for which they were educated.

CHAPTER 11

PUBLIC HEALTH AND NUTRITION EDUCATION TODAY

PUBLIC HEALTH

Nutritional personnel working in public health are employed by health agencies at the federal, state, and local levels; they conduct needs assessments to establish priorities for nutrition programs affecting certain geographical populations or categories of people, such as children or pregnant women. Dietitians develop strategies for developing nutrition services; they implement the programs, evaluate them and revise, and establish new objectives.

Beginning in the mid-1960s, public health agencies increased direct nutrition services to populations at nutrition risk or with demonstrated nutrition needs, such as pregnant women, infants, and children. Services expanded so that by 1980, approximately one-half of the nutrition personnel in local health agencies were implementing WIC (Supplemental Food Program for Women, Infants and Children), a direct service program. The federal WIC program is designed to establish a clear relation between nutrition and health care services. The purpose of the program was to provide timely prenatal care to reduce the incidence of low-birth-weight infants.

At the federal level, there is a growing need for public health nutrition professionals because there has been no sense of priorities or clear focus in maternal nutrition. Therefore, there are opportunities for professionals to become involved in program development and implementation, along with nutrition research. Research is needed to establish baseline data on the nutrition and health status of the public, with special attention to infants, children, and the elderly. At the same time, plans must be developed for the assessment of remaining vulnerable groups such as adolescents, pregnant women, the handicapped, and the unemployed.

Also, community health centers, migrant health programs, and the expansion of primary health care have established additional work environments for the public health dietitian. These work environments include directing nutrition in state and local health departments with ambulatory clients in prevention and treatment centers.

NUTRITION EDUCATION

The specialty of nutrition education provides many work environment opportunities. The two discussed here are nutrition education in the public school system and nutrition education in a fitness/health promotion program. Nutrition education in the school system may involve working for the government at the state level to expand nutrition programs or with city school districts. To work in this area, four essential categories of expertise are important. These are:

I. Nutrition and Food
   A. To provide nutrition information to individuals and groups involved in education program development
   B. To use knowledge about school foodservice to conduct nutrition-related education programs

II. Education
   A. To work with teachers and foodservice personnel to implement and evaluate nutrition programs
III. Communications
   A. To use various media (video, audio, radio) as an integral part of a nutrition education program
IV. Government
   A. To use the understanding about political processes as it relates to school food programs

The second area of nutrition education involves health promotion programs. Personal efforts to overcome smoking habits, alcohol and drug abuse, dietary excess, stress, and physical inactivity are evidence of the new health awareness in this country. As corporate America commits more resources to employee health promotion programs, due to their cost-effectiveness, more and more openings will become available for nutrition professionals to direct behavioral change programs.

The nutrition educator's roles in a fitness/health promotion program may include:

- Use of computer programs for nutrient analysis
- Interviewing to obtain diet histories
- Interpretation of biochemical tests
- Percent body fat calculation and interpretation
- Evaluation of nutritional status
- Patient counseling to determine goals
- Development of tools for recording patient progress and maintaining documentation for research
- Group counseling and education
- Development of posters and pamphlets to use as education materials
- Development of workshops to deal with behavior change, cooking techniques, restaurant eating, holidays, etc.
- Writing for lay publications

These roles may vary depending on the actual work environment; however, they are all important for any health promotion program.

The educational preparation necessary would include a B.S. or M.S. degree in nutrition with minor course in exercise physiology or another related field, such as psychology, counseling, business administration, or marketing. Also, status as a registered dietitian is important when competing for job openings. The more general knowledge and skill areas that should be acquired are given in the following list.[1]

Dietetic Curriculum Applicable to a Fitness Program

Teaching
- Health risk analysis (health hazard appraisal) dealing with the risk of cardiovascular disease, diabetes, obesity, hypertension, and poor eating habits
- Nutrition as it relates to exercise physiology
- Nutrition and the athlete—current fads and practices

Skills
- Interviewing adapted to needs
- Interpretation of anthropometric measurements such as body (fat) composition as influenced by exercise
- Use and interpretation of computerized nutrient data
- Calculation of risk based on health risk analysis
- Generation of record system compatible with existing document systems
- Counseling/follow-up while in co-participant role

---

1. Wagstaff, M. and Mattfeldt-Beman, M. The Fitness Opportunity for Dietetic Educators and Practitioners. *J. Am. Diet. Assoc.* 84:1465, 1984.

- Preparation/delivery of brief messages for impact in action-oriented setting
- Written communication through newsletters/audiovisuals
- Workshop planning and presentation based on group health needs and concerns
- Relationships with nontraditional health team (e.g., exercise physiologists)
- Promotion of dietitian's role in fitness programs
- Networking

The areas of public health nutrition and nutrition education are providing constant stimulation due to the diversity of work environments and work situations. For the dietitian not interested in the "traditional" clinical nutrition approach, these areas will continue to grow and challenge the nutrition professional to implement new ideas and programs.

CHAPTER 12

DESIGN FOR TOMORROW

The subject of nutrition has never been as popular as it is now. The general public is increasing its interest in health from a wellness standpoint. These facts help create a positive environment for the practice of dietetics.

The practice environment is changing, however. Dietitians willing to change and grow, to study hard, to keep up to date, and to choose the profession as a lifelong career will find the challenges can be met and a bright future is possible.

THE CHANGING SCENE

Six factors influence the demand for dietetic services. These include (1) socioeconomic trends; (2) public policy; (3) health values, attitudes, and behaviors; (4) technological advances; (5) competition; and (6) changes in the profession.[1]

   I. Social and economic trends are influenced by:
      A. Population demographics, which affect the supply of professionals, the needs for goods and services, and the location of clients
      B. The economic climate, which affects public funding for nutrition programs, the ability of clients to pay for the services, food pricing, and the supply of professionals

---

1. Fitz, Polly A., et al. Demand for Dietitians: Taking Control of the Future. *J. Am. Diet. Assoc.* 83:68, 1983.

    C. Health expenditures, which affect available dollars for preventive services and reimbursement policies
II. Public policy is influenced by:
    A. The existence of publicly supported nutrition and food programs
    B. The degree of regulatory control
    C. Reimbursement schedules
    D. Wage guidelines
III. Health values, attitudes, and behaviors are influenced by:
    A. The population's attitudes toward nutrition services and care
    B. Consumer-oriented decisions regarding health care
    C. Payment for nutrition services
IV. Technological advances influence:
    A. The delivery of food and services
    B. The use of communication resources and computer applications
    C. Creation of new dietetic roles
V. Competition influences:
    A. The consumers' ability to seek the dietitian for nutrition care
    B. The fees for services and the payment system
VI. Changes in the profession influence:
    A. The visibility of the dietitian
    B. The supply of dietitians
    C. The demand for nutrition services

The influence of these six areas will continue to change practice environments and expand the nutrition services required by industry, government, and the general public.

The direction of the future demand for dietitians based on the previously listed influences on the profession is presented in the table that follows. This represents the optimal scenario for future demand based on employer type.

Employer	Optimal Scenario
Nongovernment Organizations	
Health care facilities/organizations	Increase
Educational institutions	No Change
Commercial	Increase
Other (church, nonprofit, etc.)	No Change
Foodservice operations	Increase
Corporate health facilities	Increase
City or County Government	
Health care facilities/organizations	Increase
Educational institutions	No Change
State Government	
Health care facilities/organizations	Increase
Educational institutions	No Change
Federal Government	
Health care facilities/organizations	Increase
Educational institutions	No Change
Self-Employed or Partnership Dietitians or Other Health Providers (M.D., D.M.D., etc.)	Increase
Dietitians in Nontraditional Fields (Cooking Schools, Restaurants, Public Relations, Product Development)	Increase

This scenario contains a mixture of positive and negative elements. Fewer registered dietitians will be employed in hospitals, in higher education, and by government; more will have jobs in private industry, consulting practices, and noninstitutional health care facilities.

What impact will this changing scenario have on dietetic practice? The dietetic practitioner will have to be aware and progress in five major areas. These areas include:

1. Professional education
2. Research
3. Marketing of nutrition and services
4. Cost-effective health care
5. The American Dietetic Association

EDUCATION

New competencies or enhancement of current competencies will be demanded as dietitians move into advanced levels of practice. The only way other professionals will recognize a dietitian's expertise is for the dietitian to demonstrate that she or he has the knowledge and the competencies in many skill areas to perform required tasks.

For the *Clinical Dietitian Specialist,* the need will be for additional competency in biochemistry, pathophysiology, pharmacology, management (including cost/benefit analysis), computer applications to nutritional care, development of leadership skills for influencing legislation in the political arena, and professional assertiveness.

For the *Administrative Dietitian,* the need will be for competencies in cost/benefit analysis, computer applications to food service management, cooperative group purchasing, enhanced writing skills for technical and administrative reports, and development of leadership skills for influencing legislation in the political arena.

For the *Community Dietitian,* the need will be for increased emphasis on leadership for wellness programs and lifestyle change clinics and programs, an understanding of the cultural values and food habits of ethnic groups, and development of skills needed for writing grant proposals.[2]

RESEARCH

Research is becoming an essential component to document the value of nutrition services and for achieving third-party payment for services provided. Therefore, it is essential for the dietetic practitioner to develop consistent care, based on standardized protocols or criteria that have been developed for quality assurance.

Clinical, community, and administrative dietitians must be able to justify their services by documentation of both process and outcome. They should be able to clearly demonstrate that a positive change in diet will reduce risk factors, which in turn will lead to better health and economic savings. Therefore, the desired outcome of research will be to demonstrate clearly that nutrition services contribute to the quality of life and can be provided cost-effectively.

MARKETING

Many consumers are not informed about the nutrition services available to them or about dietitians who are qualified to provide the services. Individuals depend upon physicians and other allied health professionals—who are often not very knowledgeable about what dietitians do—to advise them about health and nutrition services.

---

2. Zolber, Kathleen. The President's Page. *J. Am. Diet. Assoc.* 81:594, 1982.

The dietitian must, therefore, apply marketing strategies to inform the public and other health care providers about the nutrition services available and to inform them that the dietitian is the professional educated to provide these nutrition services.

Target groups of this marketing effort should include the general public, third-party payers, specific employer and employee groups, and public policy makers. In addition, the current emphasis on health will increase the roles of the dietitian and will expand marketing of professional services, especially in preventive counseling to industry and to the public directly.

PROVISION OF COST-EFFECTIVE HEALTH CARE

Predictions for health care, in general, indicate a continued growth of alternate delivery systems, such as health maintenance organizations (HMOs). Services traditionally provided in hospitals will continue to be converted to out-of-hospital care by provision of lower levels of care in skilled nursing facilities and home health care. Corporate control of health care will continue to grow. Support of employers for employee health promotion will continue through growing numbers of wellness programs. Consumers are becoming very cost conscious and will seek quality services at a reasonable cost.

The nature of these changes taking place in health care is so fundamental as to present a threat to those who fail to respond and an opportunity to those who take action promptly.

Action by dietetic practitioners is the key. There is a need again to market nutrition services to the general public, employer/employee groups, third-party payers, prepaid health plans, and national and state public policy formulators.

Dietitians will be required to be more creative than ever before to solve the problems that practitioners face. Dietitians must demonstrate the value of their services by documenting the cost and the effectiveness of services.

As competition increases to provide cost-effective health care, the dietitian must take control of providing nutrition services as physicians, nurses, and pharmacists increase the delivery of nutrition services as part of their practice.

THE AMERICAN DIETETIC ASSOCIATION

The American Dietetic Association provides a means for the dietetic profession to identify those issues that must be addressed, to set goals that need to be accomplished, and to conduct programs that will strengthen the ability of dietitians to meet the needs of society. In doing so, the association supports the profession by enabling members to work together to achieve vital goals that are unattainable by individual efforts.

In addition, the association provides essential communication for members via:

- Publication of the *Journal*
- Providing information on topics ranging from legislation to public relations, dietetic education, etc.
- Providing data and information about specific areas of practice

The challenge to survive has become a joint responsibility. Dietitians working with the American Dietetic Association through dietetic practice groups and state and district associations must assert themselves and must work within the Code of Ethics and By-Laws established by the American Dietetic Association. It is this joint effort that will allow the previously mentioned goals to be achieved.

CHAPTER 13

PRACTITIONER INTERVIEWS

Nutrition continues to be a rapidly growing discipline ranging in content from agriculture and animal sciences to human medicine. Because of our own particular interests, training, and experience, each person in the field tends to see only a small portion of the full spectrum of nutrition. In an attempt to provide the interested student with as broad a spectrum as possible, we have interviewed dietitians who are currently practicing. They discuss: the current work environments and work roles; the education pathway followed; previous work experience; and the future.

NUTRITION CONSULTANT

Gail A. Levey, M.S., R.D.

Gail currently specializes in nutrition communication. She has reported the nutrition news weekly on WCBS-TV's "Channel 2 News at Noon" and was formerly on-air nutrition contributor to "CBS Morning News." She was the nutritionist for the "Weight Watchers Magazine" television show, now on videotape. Gail has discussed nutrition on the "Joan Rivers Show," "Today Show," "Good Morning America," "WABC-TV News," the Cable News Network, and Lifetime Television. She has appeared on television and radio stations across the country.

Gail is also a writer, and she contributes articles to major magazines, including *Parade, American Health, Good Food, Health, Seventeen, Weight Watchers Magazine,* and *Vegetarian Times.* She has researched articles for other writers, written nutrition booklets, lectured, and consulted for businesses.

Her undergraduate education was in nutritional sciences at Cornell University, and she completed her M.S. at Columbia University in nutrition and public health. She completed a six-month work experience to qualify to take the registration exam. She says, "I realized the R.D. was essential."

Gail suggests that dietitians develop in the following ways if they expect to have a varied practice:

- obtain a good nutrition/biochemistry education base
- acquire an advanced degree in a related area
- associate with good mentors and peers
- keep up-to-date with current trends and food product development
- strive to be visible in the media and outspoken at work
- develop writing skills

To achieve career goals, Gail states, "Versatility is the key to staying power. Be a dietitian but hone writing skills. Know sports nutrition and exercise physiology, too. Practice cardiovascular nutrition but know the mechanics of a stress test and how to take blood pressure. The more diverse your skills, the more valuable you become."

Maureen Serrano, R.D.

Maureen provides various nutrition services to a number of different organizations. She is the administrative director for a disease-prevention and health-promotion program, consults for specialty clinics at a university-based hospital, is a lecturer for a major airline, and provides services to children and adults who have developmental disabilities and to a large physician practice group that includes adult medicine, pediatrics, and obstetrics and gynecology. Maureen's work roles are diverse. She develops and implements programs on health promotion and disease prevention, which include body composition testing, fitness testing, computerized dietary analysis, and lifestyle assessment. She also develops menus and therapeutic diets for persons with special needs, counsels patients, and lectures on healthy eating.

Maureen obtained her B.S. degree in human nutrition and dietetics and completed a dietetic internship in order to obtain her R.D. status. This gave her a broad focus on nutrition, since her internship was a combination of administrative, clinical, and foodservice roles.

Maureen finds that her consulting business allows her the flexibility to combine her varied work experiences and interests with her goal as a wife and mother. She feels that organization is crucial to a successful business and gives the client a sense of one's expertise. Displaying a positive self-image also transmits a dedication to health, and effective communication skills transmit a clear message. In addition, networking with dietitians and other health professionals helps to establish a strong professional foundation essential for the dietitian who chooses to pursue a career as a consultant.

CURRICULUM DEVELOPMENT TEAM LEADER, THE CULINARY INSTITUTE OF AMERICA
Cathy Powers, M.S., R.D.

Cathy received her B.S. degree in dietetics from Indiana University of Pennsylvania and her M.S. degree in restaurant and hotel management at Purdue University, Indiana. She was then employed by the Culinary Institute of America in Hyde Park, New York. Her challenge was to develop a nutrition program throughout the culinary curriculum. The outcome was a restaurant concept that incorporated the nutrition principles—low fat, salt, and cholesterol; moderate protein; and high carbohydrate—with classical culinary techniques and standards. The concept eventually included computer nutrient analysis of guest menus and recipes, and a state grant provided funding for computers for student use.

Now Cathy, as well as other nutrition professionals, teach Culinary Institute students, corporate chefs, major hotel chain foodservice personnel, the military, school systems, and others how to implement nutrition concepts in the kitchen. Additionally, the Culinary Institute plans to release a nutritional cooking book, a series of videotapes, a computer analysis software package for the chef or foodservice professional, and a slide presentation.

Cathy believes that the future is food—specifically, teaching individuals how to implement nutrition principles in the kitchen. The objective is to teach chefs how to offer healthy alternatives and make them aware of portion sizes, and to educate service staff about healthy menu options.

For the dietetic student, Cathy states, "Don't be afraid to create your own path. There are opportunities waiting for the person willing to open the door and go in a route not tried before." Cathy believes that essential skills include computer knowledge, writing, public speaking, food preparation and "people-management." In addition, Cathy feels it is important to be aware of new food products and labeling standards.

NUTRITIONIST, MCDONALD'S® CORPORATION, NUTRITION AND PRODUCT DEVELOPMENT

Janet Helm, M.S., R.D.

Janet is currently the nutritionist for McDonald's Corporation. Her major role is to strengthen the nutrition function of product development in order to maintain nutrient analysis of products and to determine how to communicate nutrition information to the customer.

Janet received her B.S. degree in home economics and mass communications and her M.S. degree from Kansas State University. She then pursued a six-month work experience to qualify to take the R.D. exam, spending half of the time at a hospital and the other half at an NBC-affiliate TV station. She entered the profession as a dietetic technician at a hospital where she obtained valuable experience as a nutrition educator. She wrote for the hospital newsletter and developed patient education materials and community nutrition classes.

After her six-month work experience, Janet went on to work for the Greater Kansas City Dairy Council (affiliated with the National Dairy Council). She then became an account executive/nutrition specialist for Ketchum Public Relations in New York City. While at Ketchum, Janet worked on several food-related accounts including the National Livestock and Meat Board, the California Prune Board, American Egg Board, Hoffman La-Roche's Vitamin Nutrition Information Service, and in Ketchum's test kitchen, developing and analyzing recipes. Additionally, Janet was involved with developing press material and consumer brochures, and she organized nutrition conferences for Ketchum clients.

For the future, Janet states, "Nutrition is only going to continue to be an important issue. We must work hard to maintain traditional roles while we also build in other areas." Janet believes that nutrition opportunities are growing in the areas where the nutrition professional uses his or her skills and background in different settings, such as public relations, restaurant management, food product development, and marketing.

DIRECTOR OF NUTRITION, DIET, AND FITNESS CENTER—GOOD HOUSEKEEPING INSTITUTE

Amy Barr, M.S., R.D.

Amy is involved with clearing all advertising that has anything to do with nutrition, including food labeling, calorie content, and nutrition claims, and with checking recipes. She also writes a column called "What's News: Nutrition, Diet, and Fitness" for the Institute. In addition, she is involved in radio and TV tours that discuss current nutrition issues. The Center also provides the computer-base software information on all the recipes published in the magazine. The Center currently employs one other dietitian, a home economist, and a kitchen technician.

Amy received her B.S. in home economics with a major in nutrition at the University of Nebraska, and completed an Ed.M. degree in nutrition at Tufts University and an M.S. in science journalism at Boston University.

Amy relates that the hospital setting is not for everyone. Future job expansion includes nutrition positions in advertising, marketing, public relations, and other areas of business. She feels that additional course work in business management, advertising, and communications is important for the future nutrition professional.

NUTRITIONIST/WRITER

Virginia Aronson, M.S., R.D.

Virginia works as the nutritionist/writer for the Harvard Department of Nutrition. She writes nutrition education materials for lay individuals and professionals. She has also written nine books and writes a monthly column for *Runners World* and *Shape* magazines.

Her education began at the University of Vermont, where she received her B.S. in dietetics (a traditional program). She completed her internship in New York and received her M.S. from Framingham State University in nutrition with an emphasis in education. Following completion of her M.S. degree, she worked for the Community Health Education Department, developing and implementing weight-control clinics, group workshops, and lectures.

Virginia feels that additional course work in education, writing, and communication and practice in working with the media would be helpful to achieve a rewarding career. She perceives that a nutrition career will expand into (1) public education-related areas, such as fitness centers; (2) preventive/wellness education; and (3) nutrition writing and related communication.

MANAGER OF NUTRITION TECHNICAL SERVICES—GENERAL MILLS, INC.
Rita Warren, M.S., R.D.

Rita acts as the consultant for nutrition resources for internal groups within General Mills, Inc. Her department looks at the nutrition impact of products and nutrition labeling, and the department also discusses nutrition concerns with marketing. Other areas include providing nutrition education to health professionals via a newsletter, pamphlets, and booklets, and providing nutrition education to schools. There are ten nutritionists employed by the department. All have at least an M.S. degree and are R.D.s or R.D.-qualified.

Rita received her undergraduate degree in food science with a minor in chemistry, and her M.S. degree in nutrition with a minor in food science. She worked in the Food Chemistry lab at the University of Minnesota, then went to Pillsbury and worked on chemical analysis of foods.

Rita feels the skills that are important for future career development include knowledge about computers, communications, business, and an awareness about government nutrition policies.

TECHNICAL INFORMATION SPECIALIST— NATIONAL AGRICULTURAL LIBRARY
Carole Shore, M.S., R.D.

Carole has a unique position as a "librarian." There are only a few library staffs that she is aware of who have selected nutrition professionals and trained them in library management to provide nutrition-related services. Some of these are:

- The National Agricultural Library
- The Congressional Research Service
- The National Medical Library

There are two major work areas—acquisitions and reference. Acquisitions deals with acquiring the selection of books, journals, and audiovisuals that the library will catalog. Reference librarians are subject matter specialists who help clients receive the information they are interested in. They will also index, abstract material, and work with computers to provide short bibliographical data on nutrition topics. Carole currently works with three other registered dietitians.

Carole's educational background includes her B.S. in dietetics following a traditional program with an internship. Her M.S. degree was completed in medical dietetics at Ohio State University. Her previous work experience included research with the United States Department of Agriculture, developing United States Dietary Goals.

Carole feels the future nutrition student should choose a career that provides the potential to "ladder" or move upward in responsibility and authority. There is a need to combine two disciplines—e.g., dietetics and information science or dietetics and management. She perceives growth potential in public health and community nutrition because of the increase in hospital costs and in the aging population. Also, Carole believes that the information explosion will create a greater need in library sciences.

NUTRITION SPECIALIST/WRITER/CONSULTANT

Linda Houtkooper, Ph.D., R.D.

As a lecturer, Linda has taught undergraduate studies in nutrition as it applies to life. This work involved organizing visual aids, writing lectures, evaluating student projects and progress, and providing student counseling. As a writer, Linda currently writes for *Swimming World* magazine, where she contributes a monthly column on questions related to nutrition and swimming performance. She also writes feature nutrition articles for *Swim Magazine* and has developed videotapes titled *Winning Sports Nutrition 1: The Training Diet* and *2: The Competition Diet.* In addition to writing for lay publications, Linda has written for professional journals. A recent publication discussed body composition assessment methods for children, using bioelectrical impedance.

As a consultant, Linda has provided nutrition advice for program development at the Gatorade® Sports Sciences Institute; has provided sports nutrition information to aerobic instructors' workshops; has developed and implemented a nutrition weight management course for an employee fitness program; and has done literature review/research to update paraprofessionals.

Linda received her B.S. in home economic education with a minor in guidance and counseling. Her Ph.D. is in nutritional sciences with a minor in exercise physiology. Her research involves validation of new methods of analysis for body composition, assessment of nutritional status of elite female heptathletes, and determining the effects of resistance weight training on bone mineral content of healthy young women.

When asked about the future, Linda says that she sees nutrition evolving in interdisciplinary areas. She foresees dietitians working with behavior therapists, exercise physiologists, pharmacists, and physicians, doing research and program development for the community, in business and industry, and at universities.

PROFESSOR/NUTRITIONIST— UNIVERSITY OF ARIZONA

Mary Ann Kight, Ph.D., R.D.

Mary Ann's current area of practice involves research, development, and education related to nutritional diagnosis in the practice of R.D.s. She describes a traditional four-step care process: *Assessment, Plan, Implementation,* and *Evaluation.* She believes that for dietitians to reach a higher level of professionalism, an autonomous role or posture must be achieved. Therefore, a fifth level of care—the *Diagnostic Step,* previously performed solely by physicians and nurses—is now included in and defined as a role for the dietitian. This new role will open the door to defining clinical dietetics and its phenomenon of concern—i.e., to characterize the unique perspective or distinct way of viewing those problems that will ultimately define the limits and nature of clinical dietetics as a scientific discipline.

Dr. Kight's education background began with her B.S. in human nutrition and dietetics; her M.S. and Ph.D. degrees were in biochemistry and nutrition. She has remained in the academic environment to establish research and teaching credentials, which she felt were prerequisites to the diagnostic contribution.

For the future, Dr. Kight states, "Through the teaching of and use of the five-step care process, dietetic-specific diagnostic categories, nutritional diagnostic criteria, and nutritional diagnostic standards of practice, the R.D. will achieve an autonomous role. This will not be automatic. It will require strong continuing education programs followed by a stronger formal education."

CONCLUSION

It is exciting to learn about the variety of positions available for the nutrition professional. It is evident that career opportunities can provide a rewarding work environment and the ability to develop as a team member. A formalized education program, registration status, continuing education, and a mentor/peer group are all essential for the development of a nutrition professional.

ASSOCIATIONS

NATIONAL

American Association of Nutritional Consultants
810 S. Buffalo
Warsaw, IN 46580
(888) 828-2262
Fax: (219) 267-7006

American Celiac Society/Dietary Support Coalition
58 Musano Court
West Orange, NJ 07052-4114
(973) 325-8837
Fax: (973) 669-8808

American College of Nutrition
Hospital for Joint Diseases
301 E. Seventeenth Street
New York, NY 10003
(212) 777-1037
Fax: (212) 777-1103

American Dietetic Association
216 W. Jackson Boulevard, Suite 800
Chicago, IL 60606
(312) 899-0040
Fax: (312) 899-1979

American Society for Clinical Nutrition
9650 Rockville Pike
Bethesda, MD 20814-3998
(301) 530-7110
Fax: (301) 571-1863

American Society for Nutritional Sciences
9650 Rockville Pike
Bethesda, MD 20814-3990
(301) 530-7050
Fax: (301) 571-1892

American Society for Parenteral and Enteral Nutrition
8630 Fenton Suite, No. 412
Silver Spring, MD 20910-3805
(301) 587-6315
Fax: (301) 587-2365

Association of Vegetarian Dietitians and Nutrition Educators
3835 State Route 414
Burdett, NY 14818
(607) 546-7171
Fax: (607) 546-4091

Child Nutrition Forum
1875 Connecticut Avenue, N.W., Suite 540
Washington, DC 20009
(202) 986-2200
Fax: (202) 986-2525

Consultant Dietitians in Health Care Facilities
216 W. Jackson Boulevard, Suite 800
Chicago, IL 60606
(312) 899-0040
Fax: (312) 899-1758

Dietary Managers Association
406 Surrey Woods Drive
St. Charles, IL 60174
(630) 587-6336
Fax: (630) 587-6308

Health Care Quality Alliance
1100 Fifteenth Street, N.W.
Washington, DC 20005
(202) 835-3535
Fax: (202) 466-4243

International Academy of Nutrition and Preventive Medicine
P.O. Box 18433
Asheville, NC 28814-0433

National Association of Meal Programs
  1414 Prince Street, Suite 202
  Alexandria, VA 22314
  (703) 548-5558
  Fax: (703) 548-8024

National Perinatal Association
  3500 E. Fletcher Avenue, #209
  Tampa, FL 33613
  (813) 971-1008
  Fax: (813) 971-9306

Natural Food Associates (NFA)
  8345 Walnut Hill Lane, Suite 225
  Dallas, TX 75231-4205

Nutrition Education Association (Inc.)
  P.O. Box 20301
  3647 Glen Haven
  Houston, TX 77225
  (713) 665-2946

Nutrition Screening Initiative
  1010 Wisconsin Avenue, N.W., Suite 800
  Washington, DC 20007
  (202) 625-1662
  Fax: (202) 338-2334

Society for Nutrition Education (SNE)
  2850 Metro Drive, Suite 416
  Minneapolis, MN 55425-1412
  (612) 854-0035
  Fax: (612) 854-7869

For more information, access the American Dietetic Association at—http://www.eatright.org.

DIDACTIC PROGRAMS

Didactic Program in Dietetics (DPD) is a term used by the American Dietetic Association to describe the program approved under the standards of education as meeting course work requirements culminating in at least a bachelor's degree.

Each of the following programs is approved by the Commission on Accreditation/Approval for Dietetics Education. Graduates of these programs who are verified by the program director may apply for dietetic internships or preprofessional practice programs to establish eligibility for membership in the American Dietetic Association.

Alabama

Auburn University
Department of Nutrition and Food Science
328 Spidle Hall
Auburn University 36849-5605
(334) 844-4261
Fax: (334) 844-3268

Samford University
Department of Human Sciences and Design
800 Lakeshore Drive
Birmingham 35229-2239
(205) 870-2930
Fax: (205) 870-2068

Oakwood College
Family and Consumer Sciences
Huntsville 35896
(256) 726-7230
Fax: (256) 726-7233

Jacksonville State University
  Department of Family and Consumer Sciences
  Mason Hall
  Jacksonville 36265
  (205) 782-5054
  Fax: (205) 782-5916

University of Montevallo
  Department of Family and Consumer Sciences
  Station #6385
  Montevallo 35115-6000
  (205) 665-6385
  Fax: (205) 665-6387

Alabama A&M University
  Area of Nutrition and Hospitality Management
  Division of Family and Consumer Sciences
  Box 639
  Normal 35762
  (205) 851-5440/5498
  Fax: (205) 851-5433

The University of Alabama
  Department of Human Nutrition and Hospitality Management
  Box 870158
  Tuscaloosa 35487-0158
  (205) 348-4710
  Fax: (205) 348-3789

Tuskegee University
  Department of Home Economics
  202 Washington Hall
  Tuskegee 36088
  (334) 727-8331
  Fax: (334) 727-8493

Arizona

Northern Arizona University
  Food and Nutrition Science
  NAU Box 15095
  Flagstaff 86011-5095
  (520) 523-6164/4122
  Fax: (520) 523-0148

Arizona State University
  Department of Family Resources and Human Development
  Box 872502
  Tempe 85287-2502
  (602) 965-7731
  Fax: (602) 965-6779

University of Arizona
  Department of Nutritional Sciences
  Tucson 85721
  (520) 621-1619/9904
  Fax: (520) 621-9446

Arkansas

Ouachita Baptist University
  Department of Family and Consumer Sciences
  P.O. Box 3769
  Arkadelphia 71998-0001
  (870) 245-5542
  Fax: (870) 245-5500

University of Central Arkansas
  Department of Family and Consumer Sciences
  McAlister Hall 100
  Conway 72035-0001
  (501) 450-5950
  Fax: (501) 450-5958

University of Arkansas
  School of Human Environmental Sciences
  118 HOEC
  Fayetteville 72701
  (501) 575-4305
  Fax: (501) 575-7171

University of Arkansas at Pine Bluff
  Department of Human Services
  P.O. Box 4971
  Pine Bluff 71611
  (870) 543-8817
  Fax: (870) 543-8823

Harding University
  Department of Family and Consumer Sciences
  Box 12233
  900 E. Center Avenue
  Searcy 72149-0001
  (501) 279-4472
  Fax: (501) 279-4098

California

Pacific Union College
  Family and Consumer Sciences Department
  Angwin 94508-9797
  (707) 965-6694
  Fax: (707) 965-6390

University of California, Berkeley
  Department of Nutritional Sciences
  119 Morgan Hall
  Berkeley 94720-3104
  (510) 642-4090
  Fax: (510) 642-0535

California State University, Chico
  Department of Biological Science
  Tehama Hall, 124
  Chico 95929-0002
  (916) 898-6805
  Fax: (916) 898-4363

University of California, Davis
  Department of Nutrition
  3143 Meyer Hall
  Davis 95616-8669
  (530) 752-0160
  Fax: (530) 752-8966

California State University, Fresno
  Department of Enology, Food Science, and Nutrition
  5300 N. Campus Drive
  Fresno 93740-0017
  (209) 278-2043
  Fax: (209) 278-7623

California State University, Long Beach
Department of Family and Consumer Sciences
1250 Bellflower Boulevard
Long Beach 90840-0501
(562) 985-4545
Fax: (562) 985-4414

California State University, Los Angeles
Department of Health and Nutritional Sciences
5151 State University Drive
Los Angeles 90032-8172
(323) 343-5439
Fax: (323) 343-5598

Pepperdine University
Natural Science Division
Malibu 90263
(310) 456-4339
Fax: (310) 456-4816

California State University, Northridge
Department of Family Environmental Sciences
18111 Nordhoff Street
Northridge 91330-8308
(818) 677-3051
Fax: (818) 677-4778

California State Polytechnic University
Nutrition and Consumer Sciences
3801 W. Temple Avenue
Pomona 91768
(909) 869-2168/2226
Fax: (909) 869-5078

California State University, Sacramento
Department of Human Environmental Sciences
6000 J Street
Sacramento 95819-6053
(916) 278-6393
Fax: (916) 278-7520

California State University, San Bernardino
Department of Health Science & Human Ecology
5500 University Parkway
San Bernardino 92407-2397
(909) 880-5340
Fax: (909) 880-7037

San Diego State University
  Department of Exercise and Nutritional Sciences
  San Diego 92182-0171
  (619) 594-3045
  Fax: (619) 594-6553

San Francisco State University
  Consumer and Family Studies/Dietetics
  1600 Holloway
  San Francisco 94132
  (415) 338-6988
  Fax: (415) 338-0947

San Jose State University
  Department of Nutrition and Food Science
  San Jose 95192-0058
  (408) 924-3109
  Fax: (408) 924-3114

California Polytechnic State University
  Food Science/Nutrition Department
  San Luis Obispo 93407
  (805) 756-6126
  Fax: (805) 756-1146

Colorado

Colorado State University
  Department of Food Science and Human Nutrition
  Fort Collins 80523-1571
  (970) 491-7462
  Fax: (970) 491-7252

University of Northern Colorado
  Department of Community Health and Nutrition
  Gunter 2320
  Greeley 80639
  (970) 351-1705
  Fax: (970) 351-1489

Connecticut

University of Connecticut
  Department of Nutritional Sciences
  U-17
  3624 Horsebarn Road Extension
  Storrs 06269
  (860) 486-0119
  Fax: (860) 486-3674

St. Joseph College
  Department of Nutrition and Family Studies
  1678 Asylum Avenue
  West Hartford 06117
  (860) 232-4571
  Fax: (860) 231-8396

University of New Haven
  School of Hotel/Restaurant/Dietetics and Tourism Administration
  Department of Dietetics
  300 Orange Avenue
  West Haven 06516
  (203) 932-7413
  Fax: (203) 932-7083

Delaware

Delaware State University
  Department of Family and Consumer Sciences
  1200 N. Dupont Highway
  Dover 19901-2277
  (302) 739-4964
  Fax: (302) 739-6784

University of Delaware
  Department of Nutrition and Dietetics
  234A Alison Hall
  Newark 19716-3301
  (302) 831-8765
  Fax: (302) 831-4186

District of Columbia

University of the District of Columbia
  Department of Biological and Environmental Sciences
  4200 Connecticut Avenue, N.W.
  BLDG 44, Room-200-02
  Washington 20008
  (202) 274-5516
  Fax: (202) 274-5952

Florida

University of Florida
  Food Science and Human Nutrition Department
  359 FSB
  Gainesville 32611
  (352) 392-1991
  Fax: (352) 392-9467

University of North Florida
  College of Health
  4567 St. Johns Bluff Road, South
  Jacksonville 32224-2645
  (904) 620-2840
  Fax: (904) 620-2848

Florida International University
  Department of Dietetics and Nutrition
  HB 208 University Park
  Miami 33199
  (305) 348-2878
  Fax: (305) 348-1996

Florida State University
  Department of Nutrition, Food, and Movement Sciences
  College of Human Sciences
  Tallahassee 32306-1493
  (850) 644-4794
  Fax: (850) 644-0700

Georgia

University of Georgia
  Department of Food and Nutrition
  College of Family and Consumer Sciences
  Dawson Hall
  Athens 30602
  (706) 542-7983/4869
  Fax: (706) 542-5059

Georgia State University
  Department of Nutrition
  Box 873
  University Plaza
  Atlanta 30303-3083
  (404) 651-1108
  Fax: (404) 651-1235

Fort Valley State College
  Department of Family and Consumer Sciences
  805 State College Drive
  Fort Valley 31030
  (912) 825-6234
  Fax: (912) 825-6078

Life College
  Department of Nutrition
  1269 Barclay Circle
  Marietta 30060
  (770) 426-2736
  Fax: (770) 429-1532

Georgia Southern University
  Department of Family and Consumer Sciences
  Box 8034
  Statesboro 30460-8034
  (912) 681-5345
  Fax: (912) 681-0276

Hawaii

University of Hawaii–Manoa
  Department of Food Science and Human Nutrition
  2515 Campus Road
  Miller Hall 12 B
  Honolulu 96822
  (808) 956-3847
  Fax: (808) 956-7096

Idaho

Idaho State University
  Department of Health and Nutrition Sciences
  Box 8109
  Pocatello 83209-8109
  (208) 236-2352
  Fax: (208) 236-4903

Illinois

Southern Illinois University at Carbondale
  Department of Animal Science, Food, and Nutrition
  Mailcode 4317
  Carbondale 62901-4317
  (618) 453-7512
  Fax: (618) 453-7517

Eastern Illinois University
  School of Family and Consumer Sciences
  600 Lincoln Avenue
  Charleston 61920-3099
  (217) 581-3223/6076
  Fax: (217) 581-6090

Loyola University Chicago
  Department of Food and Nutrition
  6525 N. Sheridan Road
  Chicago 60626
  (773) 508-8299
  Fax: (773) 508-8008

Northern Illinois University
  School of Family, Consumer, and Nutrition Sciences
  DeKalb 60115-2854
  (815) 753-6384
  Fax: (815) 753-1321

Olivet Nazarene University
  Department of Family and Consumer Science
  P.O. Box 592
  Kankakee 60901-0592
  (815) 939-5398
  Fax: (815) 935-4990

Benedictine University
  Department of Biological Sciences
  5700 College Road
  Lisle 60532-0900
  (630) 829-6534
  Fax: (630) 829-6551

Western Illinois University
  Department of Family and Consumer Sciences
  Macomb 61455-1396
  (309) 298-1581
  Fax: (309) 298-2688

Illinois State University
  Family and Consumer Sciences
  Campus Box 5060
  Normal 61790-5060
  (309) 438-8850
  Fax: (309) 438-5037

Bradley University
  Family and Consumer Sciences Department
  1501 W. Bradley Avenue
  Peoria 61625
  (309) 677-2436
  Fax: (309) 677-2330

Dominican University
  Department of Nutrition Sciences
  7900 W. Division Street
  River Forest 60305
  (708) 524-6906
  Fax: (708) 366-5360

University of Illinois
  Department of Food Science and Human Nutrition
  345 Bevier Hall
  905 S. Goodwin Avenue
  Urbana 61801
  (217) 244-2884
  Fax: (217) 244-7877

Indiana

Indiana University
  Department of Applied Health Science
  HPER 116
  Bloomington 47405-4801
  (812) 855-6437
  Fax: (812) 855-3936

Marian College
  Department of Nursing and Nutrition Sciences
  Food and Nutrition Sciences Program
  3200 Cold Springs Road
  Indianapolis 46222-1997
  (317) 955-6346
  Fax: (317) 955-6448

Ball State University
  Department of Family and Consumer Sciences
  Muncie 47306-0250
  (765) 285-5931
  Fax: (765) 285-2314

Purdue University
  Department of Foods and Nutrition
  1264 Stone Hall
  West Lafayette 47907-1264
  (765) 494-8238
  Fax: (765) 494-0674

Iowa

Iowa State University
  Department of Food Science and Human Nutrition
  1104 Human Nutrition Center
  Ames 50011-1120
  (515) 294-4436
  Fax: (515) 294-6193

University of Northern Iowa
  Department of Design, Family, and Consumer Sciences
  235 Latham Hall
  Cedar Falls 50614-0332
  (319) 273-6007
  Fax: (319) 273-7096

Kansas

Kansas State University
  Department of Hotel, Restaurant, Institution Management, and Dietetics
  Department of Food and Nutrition
  Justin Hall 103
  Manhattan 66506-1404
  (913) 532-2207
  Fax: (913) 532-5522

Kentucky

Berea College
  Department of Child and Family Studies
  CPO 2319
  Berea 40404
  (606) 986-9341
  Fax: (606) 986-4506

Western Kentucky University
  Department of Consumer and Family Sciences
  Academic Complex 302F
  One Big Red Way
  Bowling Green 42101-3576
  (502) 745-4352
  Fax: (502) 745-2084

University of Kentucky
  College of Human Environmental Sciences
  Department of Nutrition and Food Science
  218 Funkhouser Building
  Lexington 40506-0054
  (606) 257-1031
  Fax: (606) 257-1675

Morehead State University
  Department of Home Economics
  P.O. 889
  Morehead 40351-1689
  (606) 783-2967
  Fax: (606) 783-5007

Murray State University
  Department of Family and Consumer Studies
  Murray 42071-0009
  (502) 762-6958
  Fax: (502) 762-6950

Eastern Kentucky University
  Home Economics Department
  102 Burrier
  Richmond 40475-3107
  (606) 622-3445/1165
  Fax: (606) 622-1163

Louisiana

Louisiana State University
  School of Human Ecology
  Baton Rouge 70803-4300
  (504) 388-2281
  Fax: (504) 388-6497

Southern University
  College of Agriculture and Home Economics
  Department of Human Nutrition and Food
  P.O. Box 11342
  Baton Rouge 70813
  (504) 771-4660
  Fax: (504) 771-3107

University of Southwestern Louisiana
  College of Applied Life Sciences
  School of Human Resources
  P.O. Box 40399
  Lafayette 70504
  (318) 482-5724
  Fax: (318) 482-5395

McNeese State University
  P.O. Box 92820
  Lake Charles 70609-2820
  (318) 475-5970
  Fax: (318) 475-5249

Louisiana Tech University
    School of Human Ecology
    P.O. Box 3167
    Ruston 71272
    (318) 257-3043
    Fax: (318) 257-4014

Nicholls State University
    Department of Family and Consumer Sciences
    Box 2014
    Thibodaux 70310
    (504) 448-4732
    Fax: (504) 449-7073

Maine

University of Maine
    Department of Food Science and Human Nutrition
    5749 Merrill Hall, Room 27
    Orono 04469-5749
    (207) 581-3130
    Fax: (207) 581-3111

Maryland

Morgan State University
    Department of Human Ecology
    Key Building #152
    Coldspring Lane and Hillen Road
    Baltimore 21239-4098
    (410) 319-3905
    Fax: (410) 319-3787

University of Maryland
    Department of Nutrition and Food Science
    College Park 20742-7521
    (301) 405-4532
    Fax: (301) 314-9327

University of Maryland, Eastern Shore
    Department of Human Ecology
    Princess Anne 21853-1299
    (410) 651-6066
    Fax: (410) 651-6207

Massachusetts

University of Massachusetts
Department of Nutrition, Box 31420
Chenoweth Laboratory
Amherst 01003-1420
(413) 545-0740
Fax: (413) 545-1074

Simmons College
Department of Nutrition
300 The Fenway
Boston 02115-5898
(617) 521-2708
Fax: (617) 521-3086

Framingham State College
Family and Consumer Sciences Department
100 State Street
Framingham 01701-9101
(508) 626-4759
Fax: (508) 626-4003

Michigan

University of Michigan
School of Public Health
Human Nutrition Program
1420 Washington Heights
Ann Arbor 48109-2029
(313) 764-3277
Fax: (313) 764-5233
(Bachelor's degree prerequisite for admission)

Andrews University
Department of Nutrition
Berrien Springs 49104-0210
(616) 471-3370
Fax: (616) 471-3485

Marygrove College
Human Ecology Department
8425 W. McNichols Road
Detroit 48221-2599
(313) 972-1322
Fax: (313) 972-1345

Michigan State University
  Department of Food Science and Human Nutrition
  2112 Anthony Hall
  East Lansing 48824-1030
  (517) 355-6483
  Fax: (517) 353-1676

Western Michigan University
  Department of Family and Consumer Sciences
  3024 Kohrman Hall
  Kalamazoo 49008
  (616) 387-3729
  Fax: (616) 387-3353

Madonna University
  Department of Biological and Health Sciences
  36600 Schoolcraft Road
  Livonia 48150-1173
  (734) 432-5534
  Fax: (734) 432-5343

Northern Michigan University
  HPER
  Marquette 49855
  (906) 227-2366
  Fax: (906) 227-2181

Central Michigan University
  Human Environmental Studies
  Wightman Hall 205
  Mt. Pleasant 48859
  (517) 774-5604
  Fax: (517) 774-2435

Minnesota

The College of St. Scholastica
  Department of Dietetics
  1200 Kenwood Avenue
  Duluth 55811-4199
  (218) 723-6101
  Fax: (218) 723-6472

Mankato State University
  Family Consumer Science Department
  MSU 44, P.O. Box 8400
  Mankato 56002-8400
  (507) 389-5923/2421
  Fax: (507) 389-2411

Concordia College
    Department of Family and Nutrition Sciences
    Moorhead 56562
    (218) 299-3748
    Fax: (218) 299-4308

The College of St. Catherine
    Family Consumer and Nutritional Sciences
    2004 Randolph Avenue
    St. Paul 55105
    (651) 690-6204
    Fax: (651) 690-6024

University of Minnesota
    Department of Food Science and Nutrition
    1334 Eckles Avenue
    St. Paul 55108-6099
    (612) 624-3255
    Fax: (612) 625-5272

Mississippi

University of Southern Mississippi
    School of Home Economics
    Box 5035
    Hattiesburg 39406-5035
    (601) 266-4679
    Fax: (601) 266-4680

Alcorn State University
    Department of Family and Consumer Sciences
    1000 ASU Drive #839
    Lorman 39096-9402
    (601) 877-6252
    Fax: (601) 877-6219

Mississippi State University
    School of Human Sciences
    Box 9746
    Mississippi State 39762-9746
    (601) 325-7702
    Fax: (601) 325-7700

University of Mississippi
    Department of Family and Consumer Sciences
    Meek Hall
    University 38677
    (601) 232-7371
    Fax: (601) 232-7039

Missouri

Southeast Missouri State University
  Department of Human Environmental Studies
  Cape Girardeau 63701-4799
  (573) 651-2994
  Fax: (573) 651-2949

Northwest Missouri State University
  College of Education and Human Services
  Department of Human Environmental Sciences
  Administration Building, Room 309
  Maryville 64468-6001
  (660) 562-1167
  Fax: (660) 562-1900

The College of the Ozarks
  Dietetics and Nutrition Education
  Point Lookout 65726
  (417) 334-6411
  Fax: (417) 335-2618

Southwest Missouri State University
  Department of Biomedical Sciences
  Springfield 65804
  (417) 836-5321/5603
  Fax: (417) 836-5588

Fontbonne College
  Department of Human Environmental Sciences
  6800 Wydown Boulevard
  St. Louis 63105-3098
  (314) 889-1415
  Fax: (314) 889-1451

St. Louis University
  School of Allied Health Professions
  Department of Nutrition and Dietetics
  3437 Caroline Street
  St. Louis 63104-1111
  (314) 577-8523

Central Missouri State University
  Department of Human Environmental Sciences
  Grinstead 235
  Warrensburg 64093-5022
  (660) 543-4217
  Fax: (660) 543-8295

Montana

Montana State University
  Department of Health and Human Development
  201 Romney
  Bozeman 59717-0336
  (406) 994-6338
  Fax: (406) 994-6314

Nebraska

University of Nebraska at Kearney
  Department of Family and Consumer Sciences
  Otto Olsen Building, Room 205C
  Kearney 68849-2130
  (308) 865-8230/8228
  Fax: (308) 865-8040

University of Nebraska, Lincoln
  Department of Nutritional Science and Dietetics
  202 Ruth Leverton Hall
  Lincoln 68583-0806
  (402) 472-4633
  Fax: (402) 472-1587

Nevada

University of Nevada, Reno
  Department of Nutrition
  Mail Stop 142
  Reno 89557-0132
  (702) 784-6446
  Fax: (702) 784-6449

New Hampshire

University of New Hampshire
  Department of Animal and Nutritional Sciences
  Human Nutrition Center
  Colovos Road
  Durham 03824
  (603) 862-1723
  Fax: (603) 862-0308

Keene State College
  Home Economics/Human Services
  Joslin House, Room 207
  Keene 03435-2903
  (603) 358-2859
  Fax: (603) 358-2257

New Jersey

College of St. Elizabeth
  Department of Foods and Nutrition
  2 Convent Road
  Morristown 07960-6989
  (973) 290-4065
  Fax: (973) 290-4676

Rutgers University
  Department of Nutritional Sciences
  Davison Hall
  26 Nichol Avenue
  New Brunswick 08901-2882
  (732) 932-9570
  Fax: (732) 932-6522

Montclair State University
  Department of Human Ecology
  Upper Montclair 07043
  (973) 655-4171
  Fax: (973) 655-7155

New Mexico

University of New Mexico
  Nutrition/Dietetics Program
  Division of Individual, Family, and Community Education
  College of Education
  Albuquerque 87131-1231
  (505) 277-6434
  Fax: (505) 277-8360

New Mexico State University
  Department of Family and Consumer Sciences
  Box 30003/MSC 3470
  Las Cruces 88003-8003
  (505) 646-1178
  Fax: (505) 646-1889

New York

Herbert H. Lehman College
  Department of Health Services, Dietetics, Food, and Nutrition
  Bedford Park Boulevard, West
  Bronx 10468-1589
  (718) 960-8775/8670
  Fax: (718) 960-8908

Brooklyn College
  Department of Health and Nutrition Sciences
  2900 Bedford Avenue
  Brooklyn 11210-2889
  (718) 951-5909/5026
  Fax: (718) 951-4670

Long Island University/C.W. Post Campus
  Health Science Department
  Brookville 11548
  (516) 299-3046
  Fax: (516) 299-3106

State University College at Buffalo
  Nutrition, Hospitality, and Fashion Department
  1300 Elmwood Avenue
  Buffalo 14222-1095
  (716) 878-4333
  Fax: (716) 878-5834

Queens College
  Department of Family, Nutrition, and Exercise Sciences
  65-30 Kissena Boulevard
  Flushing 11367-1597
  (718) 997-4150
  Fax: (718) 997-4163

Cornell University-Ithaca
  Division of Nutritional Sciences
  3M5 Martha Van Rensselaer Hall
  Ithaca 14853-4401
  (607) 255-1354
  Fax: (607) 255-0178

Cornell University-Ithaca
  School of Hotel Administration
  252 Statler Hall
  Ithaca 14853-6962
  (607) 255-3458
  Fax: (607) 255-4179

Hunter College-City University of New York
  School of Health Sciences
  Brookdale Health Science Center
  425 E. Twenty-Fifth Street
  New York 10010-2590
  (212) 481-5111
  Fax: (212) 481-7650

New York University
  Department of Nutrition and Food Studies
  35 West Fourth Street, 10th Floor
  New York 10012-1172
  (212) 998-5580
  Fax: (212) 995-4194

State University of New York at Oneonta
  Department of Human Ecology
  Oneonta 13820-4015
  (607) 436-2705
  Fax: (607) 436-3084

Plattsburgh State University of New York
  Nursing, Food, and Nutrition
  101 Broad Street
  Plattsburgh 12901-2681
  (518) 564-4222
  Fax: (518) 564-3100

Rochester Institute of Technology
  School of Food, Hotel, and Travel Management
  One Lomb Memorial Drive
  Rochester 14623-5604
  (716) 475-2352
  Fax: (716) 475-5099

Syracuse University
  Department of Nutrition and Foodservice Management
  034 Slocum Hall
  Syracuse 13244-1250
  (315) 443-2386
  Fax: (315) 443-2562

Marymount College
  Department of Human Ecology
  Marian Hall
  Tarrytown 10591-3796
  (914) 332-6559
  Fax: (914) 631-8586

Russell Sage College
  Nutrition Science Program
  Ackerman Hall
  Troy 12180-4115
  (518) 244-2048
  Fax: (518) 244-2009

North Carolina

Appalachian State University
  Department of Family and Consumer Sciences
  Boone 28608
  (828) 262-2630
  Fax: (828) 265-8620

University of North Carolina-Chapel Hill
  Department of Nutrition
  McGavran-Greenberg Hall
  CB #7400
  Chapel Hill 27599-7400
  (919) 966-7214
  Fax: (919) 966-7216

Western Carolina University
  Department of Health Sciences
  Cullowhee 28723-9054
  (828) 227-7113
  Fax: (828) 227-7446

North Carolina Central University
  Department of Human Sciences
  P.O. Box 19615
  Durham 27707
  (919) 560-6477
  Fax: (919) 560-3236

Bennett College
  Home Economics Department
  900 E. Washington Street
  Greensboro 27401-3239
  (336) 370-8795
  Fax: (336) 378-0511

North Carolina A & T State University
  Department of Home Economics
  105 Benbrow Hall
  Greensboro 27411-1064
  (336) 334-7785
  Fax: (336) 334-7265

University of North Carolina at Greensboro
  Nutrition and Foodservice Systems
  P.O. Box 26170
  Greensboro 27402-6170
  (336) 334-5313
  Fax: (336) 334-4129

East Carolina University
School of Human Environmental Sciences
Department of Nutrition and Hospitality Management
Greenville 27858-4353
(252) 328-6917
Fax: (252) 328-4276

Meredith College
Department of Human Environmental Sciences
Foods and Nutrition
3800 Hillsborough Street
Raleigh 27607-5298
(919) 760-8079
Fax: (919) 760-2819

North Dakota

North Dakota State University
Department of Food and Nutrition
College of Human Development and Education
Box 5057
Fargo 58105-5057
(701) 231-7474
Fax: (701) 231-7174

Ohio

The University of Akron
School of Family and Consumer Sciences
215 Schrank Hall South
Akron 44325-6103
(330) 972-8088
Fax: (330) 972-4934

Ohio University
School of Human and Consumer Sciences
101 A Tupper Hall
Athens 45701-2979
(740) 593-2874
Fax: (740) 593-0289

Bluffton College
Family and Consumer Sciences
280 West College Avenue
Box 896
Bluffton 45817-1196
(419) 358-3233
Fax: (419) 358-3323

Bowling Green State University
  Department of Family and Consumer Sciences
  206 Johnston Hall
  Bowling Green 43403-0254
  (419) 372-7859
  Fax: (419) 372-7854

University of Cincinnati
  Program in Dietetics and Nutrition Education
  504 Dyer Hall PO 210022
  Cincinnati 45221-0022
  (513) 556-4507
  Fax: (513) 556-2483

Case Western Reserve University
  Department of Nutrition
  10900 Euclid Avenue
  Cleveland 44106-4906
  (216) 368-2442
  Fax: (216) 368-6644

The Ohio State University
  Department of Human Nutrition and Food Management
  1787 Neil Avenue
  Columbus 43210-1295
  (614) 292-8189
  Fax: (614) 292-8880

University of Dayton
  Health and Sports Science Department
  Food and Nutrition Program
  300 College Park
  Dayton 45469-1210
  (937) 229-4240
  Fax: (937) 229-4244

Kent State University
  School of Family and Consumer Studies
  Nutrition and Dietetics Program
  Nixson Hall
  Kent 44242-0001
  (330) 672-2248/2197
  Fax: (330) 672-2194

Miami University
  Department of Physical Education, Health, and Sport Studies
  18 Phillips Hall
  Oxford 45056
  (513) 529-5036
  Fax: (513) 529-5006

Notre Dame College
  4545 College Road
  South Euclid 44121-4293
  (216) 381-1680
  Fax: (216) 381-3227

Youngstown State University
  Human Ecology Department
  One University Plaza
  Youngstown 44555-0001
  (330) 742-3346
  Fax: (330) 742-2309

Oklahoma

University of Central Oklahoma
  College of Education
  Department of Human Environmental Sciences
  Edmond 73034-5209
  (405) 341-2980
  Fax: (405) 330-3822

Langston University
  Department of Human Ecology
  308/304 Jones Hall
  Langston 73050
  (405) 466-3340/3341
  Fax: (405) 466-3364

University of Oklahoma Health Sciences Center
  College of Allied Health
  Department of Nutritional Sciences
  P.O. Box 26901
  Oklahoma City 73190
  (405) 271-2113
  Fax: (405) 271-3120

Oklahoma State University
  Nutritional Sciences Department
  HES 425
  Stillwater 74078-6141
  (405) 744-5041
  Fax: (405) 744-7113

Northeastern State University
  College of Business and Industry
  Tahlequah 74464-2399
  (918) 456-5511
  Fax: (918) 458-2337

Oregon

Oregon State University
  Nutrition and Food Management Dietetic Program
  14B Milam Hall
  Corvallis 97331-5103
  (541) 737-0960
  Fax: (541) 737-6914

Pennsylvania

Cedar Crest College
  100 College Drive
  Allentown 18104-6196
  (610) 437-4471
  Fax: (610) 606-4624

Messiah College
  Department of Natural Sciences
  Grantham 17027
  (717) 766-2511
  Fax: (717) 796-5387

Immaculata College
  Department of Fashion-Foods and Nutrition
  Box 722
  Immaculata 19345-0722
  (610) 647-4400
  Fax: (610) 251-1668

Indiana University of Pennslyvania
  Department of Food and Nutrition
  10 Ackerman Hall
  Indiana 15705-1087
  (724) 357-4440
  Fax: (724) 357-7582

Mansfield University
  Simon B. Elliott Hall
  Department of Health Sciences
  Mansfield 16933
  (717) 662-4628
  Fax: (717) 662-4111

Drexel University
    Nutrition and Food Sciences
    Thirty-Second and Chestnut Streets
    Philadelphia 19104-2875
    (215) 895-2417
    Fax: (215) 895-2421

University of Pittsburgh
    School of Health and Rehabilitation Sciences
    Room 4052 Forbes Tower
    Pittsburgh 15260
    (412) 647-1201
    Fax: (412) 647-1255

Marywood University
    Department of Nutrition and Dietetics
    2300 Adams Avenue
    Scranton 18509-1598
    (717) 348-6277
    Fax: (717) 348-1817

The Pennsylvania State University
    Nutrition Department
    College of Health and Human Development
    University Park 16802-6500
    (814) 863-2923
    Fax: (814) 863-6103

West Chester University
    H302, Department of Health
    Sturzebecker Health Sciences Center
    West Chester 19383
    (610) 436-2655
    Fax: (610) 436-2860

Puerto Rico

University of Puerto Rico
    School of Home Economics
    Box 23347, UPR Station
    Rio Piedras Campus
    San Juan 00931-3347
    (787) 764-0000
    Fax: (787) 763-4130

Rhode Island

University of Rhode Island
  Department of Food Science and Nutrition
  17 Woodward Hall
  Kingston 02881-0804
  (401) 874-5869
  Fax: (401) 874-4017

South Carolina

Clemson University
  Department of Food Science
  223 Poole Agricultural Center
  Clemson 29634-0371
  (864) 656-5690
  Fax: (864) 656-0331

South Carolina State University
  Department of Family and Consumer Sciences
  Staley Hall
  P.O. Box 7084
  300 College Avenue
  Orangeburg 29117-0001
  (803) 536-8620
  Fax: (803) 533-3686

Winthrop University
  Department of Human Nutrition
  Rock Hill 29733
  (803) 323-2101
  Fax: (803) 323-2347

South Dakota

South Dakota State University
  College of Family and Consumer Sciences
  Department Nutrition and Food Science
  P.O. Box 2275A
  Brookings 57007-0497
  (605) 688-4045
  Fax: (605) 688-4439

Mount Marty College
  Department of N.F.S.
  1105 W. Eighth Street
  Yankton 57078-3724
  (605) 668-1520
  Fax: (605) 668-1607

Tennessee

University of Tennessee at Chattanooga
  Department of Human Ecology
  202 Hunter Hall
  Chattanooga 37403-2598
  (423) 755-4550/4792
  Fax: (423) 755-4479

Tennessee Technological University
  School of Home Economics
  Box 5035
  Cookeville 38505
  (931) 372-3376
  Fax: (615) 372-3150

Carson-Newman College
  Division of Family and Consumer Sciences
  Box 71881
  Jefferson City 37760
  (423) 471-3295
  Fax: (423) 471-3502

East Tennessee State University
  Department of Applied Human Sciences
  P.O. Box 70671
  Johnson City 37614-0671
  (423) 439-4411
  Fax: (423) 439-5324

University of Tennessee
  College of Human Ecology
  Department of Nutrition, Room 229
  1215 Cumberland Avenue
  Knoxville 37996-1900
  (423) 974-6244
  Fax: (423) 974-3491

The University of Tennessee at Martin
  Department of Human Environmental Sciences
  Room 340 Gooch Hall
  Martin 38238-5045
  (901) 587-7101
  Fax: (901) 587-7106

The University of Memphis
Department of Consumer Science and Education
Memphis 38152
(901) 678-3110
Fax: (901) 678-5324

Middle Tennessee State University
Department of Human Sciences
Box 86
Murfreesboro 37132
(615) 898-2091
Fax: (615) 898-5130

David Lipscomb University
Department of Family and Consumer Sciences
3901 Granny White Pike
Nashville 37204-3951
(615) 269-1000
Fax: (615) 269-1808

Tennessee State University
Department of Family and Consumer Sciences
P.O. Box 9598
3500 John A. Merritt Boulevard
Nashville 37209-1561
(615) 963-5619
Fax: (615) 963-5033

Texas

Abilene Christian University
Department of Family and Consumer Sciences
ACU, Box 28155
Abilene 79699
(915) 674-2089
Fax: (915) 674-2086

University of Texas at Austin
Department of Human Ecology
GEA 117
Austin 78712-1097
(512) 471-7639
Fax: (512) 471-5630

Lamar University
  Department of Family and Consumer Sciences
  Box 10035
  Beaumont 77710
  (409) 880-8663
  Fax: (409) 880-8666

Texas A&M University
  Human Nutrition Section
  Department of Animal Science
  College Station 77843-2471
  (409) 845-2142
  Fax: (409) 862-2378

Texas Woman's University
  Department of Nutrition and Food Sciences
  TWU Station 425888
  Denton 76204-5888
  (817) 898-2636
  Fax: (817) 898-2634

Texas Christian University
  Department of Nutrition and Dietetics
  Box 298600
  Fort Worth 76129
  (817) 921-7309
  Fax: (817) 921-7704

Texas Southern University
  Department of Human Sciences and Consumer Sciences
  3100 Cleburne Avenue
  Houston 77004
  (713) 313-7699
  Fax: (713) 313-7228

University of Houston
  Department of Human Development and Consumer Sciences
  4800 Calhoun Road
  Houston 77204-6861
  (713) 743-4120
  Fax: (713) 743-4033

Sam Houston State University
  Food Science and Nutrition
  Huntsville 77341-2177
  (409) 294-1242
  Fax: (409) 294-4204

Texas A&M University-Kingsville
Department of Human Sciences
Campus Box 168
Kingsville 78363
(512) 593-2211
Fax: (512) 593-2230

Texas Tech University
Department of Education, Nutrition, and Restaurant, Hotel Management
Box 41162
Lubbock 79409-1162
(806) 742-3068
Fax: (806) 742-3042

Stephen F. Austin State University
Department of Human Sciences
P.O. Box 13014, SFA Station
Nacogdoches 75962-3014
(409) 468-2060
Fax: (409) 468-2140

Prairie View A&M University
Department of Human Sciences
P.O. Box 4329
Prairie View 77446-4329
(409) 857-4417/4419
Fax: (409) 857-2200

University of Incarnate Word
4301 Broadway
San Antonio 78209
(210) 829-3167
Fax: (210) 829-3153

Southwest Texas State University
Family and Consumer Sciences
San Marcos 78666-4616
(512) 245-2482
Fax: (512) 245-3829

Tarleton State University
Department of Human Sciences
Box T-0380
Stephenville 76402
(254) 968-9196
Fax: (254) 968-9728

Baylor University
Department of Family and Consumer Sciences
BU Box 97346
Waco 76798-7346
(254) 710-3626
Fax: (254) 710-3629

Utah

Brigham Young University
Food Science and Nutrition Department
S219 ESC
P.O. Box 24620
Provo 84602-4620
(801) 378-6676
Fax: (801) 378-8714

Vermont

University of Vermont
Department of Nutritional Sciences
Terrill Hall
Burlington 05405-0148
(802) 656-0539
Fax: (802) 656-0407

Virginia

Virginia Polytechnic Institute & State University
Department of Human Nutrition, Foods, and Exercise
College of Human Resources and Education
Blacksburg 24061-0430
(540) 231-4672
Fax: (540) 231-3916

James Madison University
Department of Dietetics/Health Sciences
MSC 1202
Moody Hall 213A
Harrisonburg 22807
(540) 568-6362
Fax: (540) 568-8166

Norfolk State University
Food Science and Nutrition/Chemistry
2401 Corprew Avenue
Norfolk 23504-3992
(757) 683-9532
Fax: (757) 683-2909

Virginia State University
    Department of Human Ecology
    Box 9211
    Petersburg 23806
    (804) 524-5502
    Fax: (804) 524-5048/5738

Radford University
    Foods and Nutrition
    P.O. Box 6962
    Radford 24142
    (540) 831-5542
    Fax: (540) 831-6719

Washington

Bastyr University
    14500 Juanita Drive Northeast
    Bothell 98011-4995
    (425) 602-3124
    Fax: (425) 823-6222

Central Washington University
    Department of Family and Consumer Sciences
    Ellensburg 98926-7565
    (509) 963-2366
    Fax: (509) 963 2787

Washington State University
    College of Agriculture and Home Economics
    Department of Food Science and Human Nutrition
    Pullman 99164-6376
    (509) 335-1395
    Fax: (509) 335-4815

Seattle Pacific University
    Department of Family and Consumer Sciences
    3307 Third Avenue West
    Seattle 98119
    (206) 281-2708/2195
    Fax: (206) 281-2035

University of Washington
    305 Raitt Hall, Box 353410
    Seattle 98195-3410
    (206) 543-1730
    Fax: (206) 685-1696

West Virginia

West Virginia Wesleyan College
  Department of Human Ecology
  Haymond Hall 215E
  Box 15
  Buckhannon 26201-2995
  (304) 473-8379
  Fax: (304) 473-8187

Marshall University
  Family and Consumer Sciences
  Huntington 25755-2460
  (304) 696-2507/2386
  Fax: (304) 696-3177

West Virginia University
  Division of Family Resources
  College of Agriculture and Forestry
  Box 6124, Allen Hall
  Morgantown 26506-6122
  (304) 293-3402
  Fax: (304) 293-2750

Wisconsin

University of Wisconsin-Green Bay
  Department of Human Biology
  2420 Nicolet Drive
  Green Bay 54311-7001
  (920) 465-2332 or (920) 465-2681
  Fax: (920) 465-2769

University of Wisconsin-Madison
  Department of Nutritional Sciences
  1415 Linden Drive
  Madison 53706-1571
  (608) 262-4386
  Fax: (608) 262-5860

University of Wisonsin-Stout
  Dietetics Program
  College of Human Development
  Menomonie 54751-0790
  (715) 232-2994/2183
  Fax: (715) 232-2366

University of Wisconsin-Stevens Point
 School of Health Promotion and Human Development
 Stevens Point 54481-3897
 (715) 346-4087
 Fax: (715) 346-3751

Wyoming

University of Wyoming
 Department of Family and Consumer Sciences
 Laramie 82071-3354
 (307) 766-4145
 Fax: (307) 766-3379

For more information, access the American Dietetic Association at—http://www.eatright.org.

COORDINATED UNDERGRADUATE PROGRAMS

The coordinated program provides for the integration of academic course work with a minimum of nine hundred hours of supervised practice within a program granting at least a bachelor's degree.

Each program is accredited by the Commission on Accreditation/ Approval for Dietetics Education and meets the minimum academic and supervised practice requirements established to be eligible for the registration examination for dietitians.

Following is a list of the currently accredited coordinated programs.

Alabama

The University of Alabama
Department of Human Nutrition and Hospitality Management
P.O. Box 870158
Tuscaloosa 35487-0158
(205) 348-6157
Fax: (205) 348-3789

California

Loma Linda University
School of Allied Health Professions
Department of Nutrition and Dietetics
Loma Linda 92350
(909) 824-4593
Fax: (909) 824-4291

Loma Linda University
  School of Public Health
  Nutrition and Dietetics
  Loma Linda 92350
  (909) 558-4598 or (800) 422-4558
  Fax: (909) 558-4087

California State University, Los Angeles
  Department of Health and Nutritional Sciences
  5151 State University Drive
  Los Angeles 90032-8172
  (323) 343-5439
  Fax: (323) 343-2670

Charles R. Drew University of Medicine and Science
  College of Allied Health
  1731 E. 120th Street
  Los Angeles 90059
  (213) 563-4811
  Fax: (213) 563-4923

Connecticut

The University of Connecticut
  School of Allied Health
  358 Mansfield Road U-101
  Storrs 06269-2101
  (860) 486-0016
  Fax: (860) 486-1588

Saint Joseph College
  Department of Nutrition and Family Studies
  1678 Asylum Avenue
  W. Hartford 06117
  (860) 232-4571
  Fax: (860) 231-8396

District of Columbia

Howard University
  Department of Nutritional Sciences
  Division of Allied Health Sciences
  Sixth and Bryant Streets, N.W., Annex I
  Washington 20059
  (202) 806-5649/6238
  Fax (202) 806-9233

Florida

Florida International University
  Department of Dietetics and Nutrition
  Health Building, Room 201
  University Park
  Miami 33199
  (305) 348-2878
  Fax: (305) 348-1996

Idaho

University of Idaho
  School of Family and Consumer Sciences
  College of Agriculture
  Moscow 83844-3183
  (208) 885-6026 or 6546
  Fax: (208) 885-5751

Illinois

University of Illinois at Chicago
  Department of Human Nutrition and Dietetics (M/C 517)
  1919 W. Taylor Street
  Chicago 60612-7256
  (312) 996-1209
  Fax: (312) 413-0319

Indiana

Marian College
  Department of Nursing and Nutrition Sciences
  3200 Cold Spring Road
  Indianapolis, IN 46222-1997
  (317) 955-6346
  Fax: (317) 955-6448

Indiana State University
  Department of Family and Consumer Sciences
  Terre Haute 47809
  (812) 237-3309
  Fax: (812) 237-3304

Purdue University
  Department of Foods and Nutrition
  1264 Stone Hall
  West Lafayette 47907-1264
  (765) 494-8236
  Fax: (765) 494-0674

Kansas

Kansas State University
  Department of Hotel, Restaurant, Institution Management and Dietetics
  Justin Hall 103
  Manhattan 66506-1404
  (913) 532-2216
  Fax: (913) 532-5522

Kentucky

University of Kentucky
  Nutrition and Food Science
  204 Funkhouser
  Lexington 40506-0054
  (606) 257-4146
  Fax: (606) 257-3707

Massachusetts

Framingham State College
  Department of Family and Consumer Sciences
  100 State Street
  Framingham 01701-9101
  (508) 626-4754
  Fax: (508) 626-4003

Michigan

Wayne State University
  Department of Nutrition and Food Science
  3009 Science Hall
  Detroit 48202
  (313) 577-2500
  Fax: (313) 577-8616

Eastern Michigan University
  Department of Human, Environmental, and Consumer Resources
  206H Roosevelt Hall
  Ypsilanti 48197
  (313) 487-3685
  Fax: (313) 484-0575

Minnesota

College of St. Benedict/St. John's University
  Nutrition Department
  154 Ardolf Science Center
  37 S. College Avenue
  St. Joseph 56374-2099
  (320) 363-5057
  Fax: (320) 363-5582

University of Minnesota
  269 Food Science and Nutrition
  1334 Eckles Avenue
  St. Paul 55108-6099
  (612) 624-9278
  Fax: (612) 625-5272

Mississippi

University of Southern Mississippi
  Nutrition and Dietetics
  College of Health–Human Sciences
  Box 5035
  Hattiesburg 39406-5035
  (601) 266-4679
  Fax: (601) 266-4680

Missouri

University of Missouri-Columbia
  Dietetic Education
  318 Clark Hall
  Columbia 65211
  (573) 884-4137
  Fax: (573) 884-4885

New Jersey

University of Medicine and Dentistry of New Jersey
  School of Health Related Professions
  65 Bergen Street
  Newark 07107-3001
  (973) 972-6245
  Fax: (973) 972-7028

New York

D'Youville College
  320 Porter Avenue
  Buffalo 14201-1084
  (716) 881-3200
  Fax: (716) 881-7790

State University College at Buffalo
  Nutrition, Hospitality, and Fashion Department
  1300 Elmwood Avenue
  Buffalo 14222-1095
  (716) 878-5634
  Fax: (716) 878-5834

Rochester Institute of Technology
  School of Food, Hotel, and Travel Management
  George Eastman Building
  14 Lomb Memorial Drive
  Rochester 14623-5604
  (716) 475-2357
  Fax: (716) 475-5099

Syracuse University
  Department of Nutrition and Foodservice Management
  034 Slocum Hall
  Syracuse 13244-1250
  (315) 443-4789
  Fax: (315) 443-2562

North Carolina

University of North Carolina
  McGavran-Greenberg Hall
  Department of Nutrition
  CB #7400
  Chapel Hill 27599-7400
  (919) 966-7214
  Fax: (919) 966-7216

North Dakota

North Dakota State University
  Department of Food and Nutrition
  EML Hall 351
  Fargo 58105-5057
  (701) 231 7180
  Fax: (701) 231-7474

University of North Dakota
  Department of Nutrition and Dietetics
  Box 8237, University Station
  Grand Forks 58202-8237
  (701) 777-3752
  Fax: (701) 777-3650

Ohio

The University of Akron
  School of Home Economics and Family Ecology
  215 Schrank Hall South
  Akron 44325-6103
  (330) 972-6046/7721
  Fax: (330) 972-4934

The Ohio State University
School of Allied Medical Professions
1583 Perry Street
Columbus 43210-1234
(614) 292-0635
Fax: (614) 292-0210

Youngstown State University
One University Plaza
Youngstown 44555-0001
(330) 742-2309
Fax: (330) 652-3683

Oklahoma

University of Oklahoma Health Sciences Center
College of Allied Health
Department of Nutritional Sciences
Coordinated Program in Clinical Dietetics
P.O. Box 26901
Oklahoma City 73190
(405) 271-2113
Fax: (405) 271-3120

Pennsylvania

Edinboro University of Pennsylvania
Department of Biology and Health Services
Edinboro 16444
(814) 732-2458/2500

Gannon University
College of Sciences, Engineering and Health Sciences
109 University Square
Erie 16541-0001
(814) 871-5452
Fax: (814) 871-5662

Mercyhurst College
Department of Human Ecology
501 E. Thirty-Eighth Street
Erie 16546-0001
(814) 824-2462
Fax: (814) 824-2438

Seton Hill College
Division of Management, Family, and Consumer Sciences
Greensburg 15601-1599
(724) 830-1045
Fax: (724) 830-4203

University of Pittsburgh
  School of Health and Rehabilitation Sciences
  Room 4052 Forbes Tower
  Pittsburgh 15260
  (412) 647-1201
  Fax: (412) 647-1255

Marywood University
  Department of Nutrition and Dietetics
  2300 Adams Avenue
  Scranton 18509-1598
  (717) 348-6277
  Fax: (717) 348-1817

Texas

The University of Texas at Austin
  Department of Human Ecology, A2700
  Austin 78712-1097
  (512) 471- 4934
  Fax: (512) 471-5630

The University of Texas Southwestern Medical Center
  Southwestern Allied Health Sciences School
  Department of Clinical Nutrition
  5323 Harry Hines Boulevard
  Dallas 75235-8877
  (214) 648-1520
  Fax: (214) 648-1514

The University of Texas–Pan American
  College of Health Sciences and Human Services
  1201 W. University Drive
  Edinburg 78539-2999
  (956) 381-2294
  Fax: (956) 384-5054

Texas Christian University
  Department of Nutrition and Dietetics
  TCU Box 298600
  Forth Worth 76129
  (817) 257-7309
  Fax: (817) 257-7704

Utah

Utah State University
  Department of Nutrition and Food Sciences
  Logan 84322-8700
  (801) 797-2105
  Fax: (801) 797-2379

University of Utah
  College of Health
  Division of Foods and Nutrition
  239N-HPER
  Salt Lake City 84112
  (801) 581-6730
  Fax: (801) 585-3874

Washington

Washington State University
  FSHN Building 106F
  P.O. Box 646376
  Pullman 99164-6376
  (509) 335-1395
  Fax: (509) 335-4815

Wisconsin

Viterbo College
  Nutrition and Dietetics Department
  815 S. Ninth Street
  LaCrosse 54601-4797
  (608) 796-3660
  Fax: (608) 796-3030

University of Wisconsin-Madison
  Department of Nutritional Sciences
  1415 Linden Drive
  Madison 53706-1571
  (608) 262-5847
  Fax: (608) 262-5860

Mount Mary College
  Department of Dietetics
  2900 N. Menomonee River Parkway
  Milwaukee 53222-4597
  (414) 256-1216
  Fax: (414) 256-1224

For more information, access the American Dietetic Association at—http://www.eatright.org

DIETETIC TECHNICIAN PROGRAMS

The following programs (like the undergraduate programs in Appendix B) combine course work with supervised practice. These programs, however, require fewer hours of supervised practice; graduates of these programs will have earned at least an associate's degree.

Following is a list of accredited/approved dietetic technician programs. Contact the school of your choice for further information or an enrollment application.

Arizona

Central Arizona College
    8470 N. Overfield Road
    Coolidge 85228
    (520) 426-4497
    Fax: (520) 426-4476

Arkansas

Black River Technical College
    P.O. Box 468
    Pocahontas 72455
    (501) 892-4565
    Fax: (501) 892-3546

California

Orange Coast College
    2701 Fairview Road
    Costa Mesa 92628-0120
    (714) 432-5835
    Fax: (714) 432-5609

Grossmont College
  8800 Grossmont College Drive
  El Cajon 92020-1799
  (619) 465-1700
  Fax: (619) 461-3396

Loma Linda University
  Department of Nutrition & Dietetics
  School of Allied Health Professions
  Loma Linda 92350
  (714) 824-4593
  Fax: (909) 824-4291

Long Beach City College
  Liberal Arts Campus
  Family and Consumer Studies Division
  4901 E. Carson Street
  Long Beach 90808
  (562) 938-4550
  Fax: (562) 938-4118

Los Angeles City College
  Family and Consumer Studies
  855 North Vermont Avenue
  Los Angeles 90029-3590
  (323) 953-4259
  Fax: (323) 953-4294

Chaffey College
  Food Service Management
  5885 Haven Avenue
  Rancho Cucamonga 91737-3002
  (909) 941-2711
  Fax: (909) 466-2831

San Bernardino Valley College
  Family and Consumer Science
  701 South Mount Vernon
  San Bernardino 92410
  (909) 888-6511
  Fax: (909) 881-8016

Colorado

Front Range Community College
  3645 W. 112th Avenue
  Westminster 80030
  (303) 404-5260
  Fax: (303) 404-2178

Connecticut

Gateway Community Technical College
88 Bassett Road
North Haven 06473
(203) 234-3309
Fax: (203) 234-3353

Briarwood College
2279 Mount Vernon Road
Southington 06489
(860) 628-4751
Fax: (860) 628-6444

Florida

Florida Community College at Jacksonville-North Campus
4501 Capper Road
Jacksonville 32218
(904) 766-6743
Fax: (904) 766-6654

Palm Beach Community College
Dietetic Technician Program
4200 Congress Avenue
Mail Station 32
Lake Worth 33461-4796
(561) 439-8126
Fax: (561) 439-8314

Miami-Dade Community College
Mitchell Wolfson
300 N.E. Second Avenue
Miami 33132-2297
(305) 237-3160
Fax: (305) 237-7429

Pensacola Junior College
1000 College Boulevard
Pensacola 32504-8998
(904) 484-2531
Fax: (904) 484-1114

Illinois

Malcolm X College
1900 W. Van Buren
Chicago 60612-3145
(312) 850-7383
Fax: (312) 850-7453

William Rainey Harper College
   1200 W. Algonquin Road
   Palatine 60067-7398
   (847) 925-6537
   Fax: (847) 925-6047

Indiana

Purdue University–Calumet
   Behavioral Sciences Department
   2200 169th Street
   Hammond 46323-2094
   (219) 989-2716
   Fax: (219) 989-2008

Ball State University
   Department of Family and Consumer Sciences
   150 Applied Technology
   Muncie 47306
   (765) 285-2255
   Fax: (765) 285-2314

Louisiana

Delgado Community College
   450 S. Claiborne Avenue
   New Orleans 70112-1310
   (504) 568-6994
   Fax: (504) 568-5494

Maine

Southern Maine Technical College
   Fort Road
   South Portland 04106
   (207) 767-9606
   Fax: (207) 767-2731

Maryland

Baltimore City Community College
   Department of Allied Health
   2901 Liberty Heights Avenue
   Baltimore 21215-7893
   (410) 462-7724
   Fax: (410) 462-7785

Massachusetts

Laboure College
  2120 Dorchester Avenue
  Boston 02124-5698
  (617) 296-8300
  Fax: (617) 296-7947

Essex Agricultural and Technical Institute
  562 Maple Street
  Hathorne 01937
  (508) 774-0050
  Fax: (508) 774-6530

Michigan

Wayne County Community College
  Dietetic Technology Program
  8551 Greenfield Road
  Detroit 48228
  (313) 943-4074
  Fax: (313) 943-4025

Minnesota

Normandale Community College
  9700 France Avenue S.
  Bloomington 55431
  (612) 832-6481
  Fax: (612) 832-6571

University of Minnesota–Crookston
  Management Division
  2900 University Avenue
  Crookston 56716-5001
  (218) 281-8202
  Fax: (218) 281-8050

Missouri

St. Louis Community College at Florissant Valley
  3400 Pershall Road
  St. Louis 63135-1499
  (314) 595-4426
  Fax: (314) 595-2047

Nebraska

Southeast Community College
8800 "O" Street
Lincoln 68520-1227
(402) 437-2465
Fax: (402) 437-2404

Nebraska Methodist College
Metropolitan Community Consortium
8501 W. Dodge Road
Omaha 68114
(402) 354-4829
Fax: (402) 354-8875

New Hampshire

University of New Hampshire
Thompson School of Applied Science
Cole Hall
Durham 03824
(603) 862-1050
Fax: (603) 862-2915

New Jersey

Camden County College
P.O. Box 200
Blackwood 08012
(609) 227-7200
Fax: (609) 374-4880

Middlesex County College
2600 Woodbridge Avenue
P.O. Box 3050
Edison 08818-3050
(732) 906-2538
Fax: (908) 561-1885

New York

Genesee Community College
One College Road
Batavia 14020-9704
(716) 345-6870
Fax: (716) 343-0433

LaGuardia Community College
  City University of New York
  31-10 Thomson Avenue
  Long Island City 11101
  (718) 482-5758
  Fax: (718) 482-5599

State University of New York
  Agriculture and Technical College
  Bailey Annex
  Morrisville 13408
  (315) 684-6288
  Fax: (315) 684-6592

Dutchess Community College
  53 Pendell Road
  Poughkeepsie 12601-1595
  (914) 431-8323
  Fax: (914) 431-8991

Suffolk County Community College
  Eastern Campus
  121 Speonk-Riverhead Road
  Riverhead 11901-3499
  (516) 548-2590
  Fax: (516) 548-2617

Rockland Community College
  145 College Road
  Suffern 10901-3699
  (914) 574-4130
  Fax: (914) 574-4498

Westchester Community College
  75 Grasslands Road
  Valhalla 10595-1698
  (914) 785-6750
  Fax: (914) 785-6423

Erie Community College
  North Campus
  6205 Main Street
  Williamsville 14221-7095
  (716) 851-1598
  Fax: (716) 851-1429

Ohio

Cincinnati State Technical and Community College
  Health Technologies Division
  3520 Central Parkway
  Cincinnati 45223-2690
  (513) 569-1685
  Fax: (513) 569-1659

Cuyahoga Community College
  2900 Community College Avenue
  Cleveland 44115
  (216) 987-4497
  Fax: (216) 987-4386

Columbus State Community College
  550 E. Spring Street
  P.O. Box 1609
  Columbus 43216-1609
  (614) 227-2580
  Fax: (614) 227-5973

Sinclair Community College
  444 W. Third Street
  Dayton 45402-1460
  (937) 512-2756
  Fax: (937) 512-3092

Lima Technical College
  4240 Campus Drive
  Lima 45804-3597
  (419) 995-8328
  Fax: (419) 995-8818

Hocking Technical College
  3301 Hocking Parkway
  Nelsonville 45764-9704
  (614) 753-3591
  Fax: (614) 753-5105

Owens Community College
  P.O. Box 10000
  Toledo 43699-1947
  (419) 661-7218
  Fax: (419) 661-7251

Youngstown State University
  Department of Human Ecology
  One University Plaza
  Cushwa Hall, Room 3048
  Youngstown 44555-3344
  (330) 742-3345
  Fax: (330) 742-2309

Muskingum Area Technical College
  Division Health, Public Services and General Studies
  1555 Newark Road
  Zanesville 43701
  (740) 454-2501
  Fax: (740) 454-0035

Oklahoma

Oklahoma State University–Okmulgee
  1801 E. Fourth Street
  Okmulgee 74447-3901
  (918) 756-6211
  Fax: (918) 756-1315

Oregon

Portland Community College
  12000 S.W. Forty-Ninth
  P.O. Box 19000
  Portland 97280-0990
  (503) 977-4029
  Fax: (503) 977-4869

Pennsylvania

Community College of Philadelphia
  1700 Spring Garden Street
  Philadelphia 19130-3991
  (215) 751-8427
  Fax: (215) 751-8937

Community College of Allegheny County
  Allegheny Campus
  808 Ridge Avenue
  Pittsburgh 15212-6097
  (412) 237-2640
  Fax: (412) 237-4521

The Pennsylvania State University
   College of Health and Human Development
   School of Hotel, Restaurant, and Recreation Management
   University Park 16802-1307
   (814) 863-2676
   Fax: (814) 863-4257

Westmoreland County Community College
   Commissioners Hall
   Armbrust Road
   Youngwood 15697-1895
   (724) 925-4235
   Fax: (724) 925-4293

South Carolina

Greenville Technical College
   ET13A
   P.O. Box 5616
   Greenville 29606-5616
   (864) 250-8098
   Fax: (864) 250-8500

Tennessee

Shelby State Community College
   P.O. Box 40568
   Memphis 38174-0568
   (901) 544-5673 or (901) 544-5051
   Fax: (901) 544-5057

Texas

Tarrant County Junior College
   2100 TCJC Parkway
   Arlington 76018
   (817) 515-3609
   Fax: (817) 515-3179

El Paso Community College
   100 West Rio Grande Avenue
   El Paso 79902
   (915) 831-4470
   Fax: (915) 831-4114

San Jacinto College Central
8060 Spencer Highway
P.O. Box 2007
Pasadena 77501-2007
(281) 476-1501
Fax: (281) 478-2790

St. Philip's College
1801 Martin Luther King
San Antonio 78203-2098
(210) 531-3315
Fax: (210) 531-3351

Virginia

Northern Virginia Community College
HRI/DIT McDiarmid Building
8333 Little River Turnpike
Annadale 22003-3796
(703) 323-3458
Fax: (703) 323-3015

J. Sargeant Reynolds Community College
P.O. Box 85622
Richmond 23285-5622
(804) 786-8006
Fax: (804) 786-5465

Tidewater Community College
1700 College Crescent
Virginia Beach 23456
(757) 822-7336
Fax: (757) 822-1338

Washington

Shoreline Community College
16101 Greenwood Avenue N.
Seattle 98133
(206) 546-4673
Fax: (206) 546-5869

Spokane Community College
N. 1810 Greene Street, MS 2090
Spokane 99207-5399
(509) 533-7314
Fax: (509) 533-8621

Wisconsin

Madison Area Technical College
   3550 Anderson Street
   Madison 53704-2599
   (608) 246-6319
   Fax: (608) 246-6880

Milwaukee Area Technical College
   West Campus
   1200 S. Seventy-First Street
   West Allis 52314-3110
   (414) 456-5364
   Fax: (414) 456-5425

For more information, access the American Dietetic Association at—http://www.eatright.org.

PREPROFESSIONAL PRACTICE PROGRAMS (AP4)

The preprofessional practice program provides a minimum of nine hundred hours of supervised practice. Programs follow completion of at least a bachelor's degree and course work requirements. Programs are usually completed in nine to twenty-four months, depending on the availability of a part-time schedule or requirement of graduate credit.

Listed below are the currently approved preprofessional practice programs.

Alabama

Oakwood College
Family and Consumer Sciences
Oakwood Road
Huntsville 35896
(256) 726-7228
Fax: (256) 726-7233

Alaska

University of Alaska Anchorage
3211 Providence Drive
Anchorage 99508-8357
(907) 786-1362
Fax: (907) 786-1402

Arizona

Focus on Nutrition
   3923 E. Thunderbird Road, Suite 26-113
   Phoenix 85032
   (602) 788-7096
   Fax: (602) 404-8596

Paradise Valley Unified School District
   20621 N. Thirty-Second Street
   Phoenix 85024
   (602) 493-6330
   Fax: (602) 493-6334

Walter O. Boswell Memorial Hospital
   10401 W. Thunderbird Boulevard
   Sun City 85372
   (602) 977-7211
   Fax: (602) 876-5494

Arizona State University
   Department of Family Resources and Human Development
   Box 872502
   Tempe 85287-2502
   (602) 965-7034
   Fax: (602) 965-6779

Maricopa County
   Department of Public Health
   Office of Nutrition Services–AP4
   1414 W. Broadway, Suite 237
   Tempe 85282
   (602) 966-3090
   Fax: (602) 966-3233

California

University of California Berkeley
   Department of Nutritional Sciences
   119 Morgan Hall
   Berkeley 94720-3104
   (510) 642-4090
   Fax: (510) 642-0535

ARAMARK Healthcare Support Services
  2600 Michelson, Suite 1170
  Irvine 92612
  (714) 261-5168
  Fax: (714) 261-5254

Connecticut

Danbury Hospital
  24 Hospital Avenue
  Danbury 06810
  (203) 797-7816
  Fax: (203) 797-7619

Florida

The University of North Florida
  College of Health
  Department of Health Science
  4567 St. Johns Bluff Road South
  Jacksonville 32224
  (904) 646-2840
  Fax: (904) 646-2848

Georgia

University of Georgia
  Department of Foods and Nutrition
  Dawson Hall
  Athens 30602-3622
  (706) 542-4908
  Fax: (706) 542-5059

Indiana

Purdue University Calumet
  Department of Behavioral Sciences
  2200 169th Street
  Hammond 46323-2094
  (219) 989-2940
  Fax: (219) 989-2008

Kentucky

Morehead State University
  Department of Home Economics
  UPO Box 889
  Morehead 40351-1689
  (606) 783-2966
  Fax: (606) 783-5007

Maryland

University of Maryland Eastern Shore
  Department of Human Ecology
  Princess Anne 21853
  (410) 651-6066
  Fax: (410) 651-6207

Massachusetts

Sodexho Marriott Services
  153 Second Avenue
  Waltham 02254
  (800) 926-7429
  Fax: (617) 466-8709

Michigan

University of Michigan Hospitals
  C333 MedInn Building, Box 0832
  1500 E. Medical Center Drive
  Ann Arbor 48109-0832
  (313) 763-6170
  Fax: (313) 763-6426

Andrews University
  Department of Nutrition
  Berrien Springs 49104-0210
  (616) 471-3370
  Fax: (616) 471-3485

New Jersey

Montclair State University
  Department of Human Ecology
  Upper Montclair 07043
  (973) 655-4373
  Fax: (973) 655-4399

New York

Lehman College
  The City University of New York
  Department of Health Services
  Bedford Park Boulevard West
  Bronx 10468-1539
  (718) 960-8084
  Fax: (718) 960-8908

Brooklyn College
  Department of Health and Nutrition Sciences
  2900 Bedford Avenue
  Brooklyn 11210-2889
  (718) 951-5909/5026
  Fax: (718) 951-4670

The Long Island College Hospital
  Nutrition and Food Service Department
  Atlantic Avenue and Hicks Street
  Brooklyn 11201
  (718) 780-1251/1252
  Fax: (718) 780-1819

Sodexho Marriott Services-Metropolitan
  New York AP4 Program
  90 Merrick Avenue, Suite 210
  East Meadow 11554
  (516) 794-9150

Golden Hill Health Care Center
  99 Golden Hill Drive
  Kingston 12401-6442
  (914) 340-3990
  Fax: (914) 340-3828

ARAMARK Healthcare Support Services
  Metropolitan New York AP4
  Mount Sinai Medical Center
  One Gustave L. Levy Place
  Box 1066
  New York 10029
  (212) 241-0069 or (212) 241-6199

Hunter College
    Nutrition and Food Science Program
    School of Health Sciences
    425 E. Twenty-Fifth Street
    New York 10010-2590
    (212) 481-7563
    Fax: (212) 481-7650

Pennsylvania

The Wood Company
    6081 Hamilton Boulevard
    P.O. Box 3501
    Allentown 18106-0501
    (800) 545-7710
    Fax: (610) 366-5454

South Dakota

South Dakota University Affiliated Program
    The University of South Dakota School of Medicine
    414 E. Clark Street
    Vermillion 57069-2390
    (605) 677-5311
    Fax: (605) 677-6274

Texas

Lamar University
    Department of Family and Consumer Sciences
    P.O. Box 10035
    Beaumont 77710
    (409) 880-8663
    Fax: (409) 880-8666

Stephen F. Austin State University
    SFA Station 13014
    Nacogdoches 75962-3014
    (409) 468-4502
    Fax: (409) 468-2140

Wisconsin

University of Wisconsin Hospital and Clinics
   Food and Nutrition Services F4/120
   600 Highland Avenue
   Madison 53792
   (608) 263-8237
   Fax: (608) 263-0343

For more information, access the American Dietetic Association at—http://www.eatright.org.